RISE + HUSTLE

Praises for Rise and Hustle

"Just writing to let you know how "Rise and Hustle" has impacted my life. Most significantly, an attitude of gratitude. When I'm feeling depressed or overwhelmed by life or work or whatever, I just start thanking God for all His blessings on me and that really helps put things in perspective, so thanks for those reminders. I appreciate the biblical applications you make and often feel encouraged by the Scriptures you reference. I've been able to share some of your spiritual lessons with friends and family in order to encourage them. Finally, the corny jokes you sometimes include usually, at least, make me smile and people should smile more :)"

—Jesseca Church, Attorney

"As a business owner, husband, and father, there are plenty of days I'd love to hit the snooze button in the morning or skip going to the gym. And, especially during the long Wisconsin winters, my motivation can hit an all-time low pretty easily. However, after coming across Mike's incredible story, and his powerful 90-second daily rituals, my life has been better than ever. In less than two minutes, I'm in the right frame of mind to attack the day, focus on what's important, and take massive action toward my goals and dreams. It'll do the same for you."

—Derek Wahler, author of the *Fat Shrinking Signal*

"People are exhausted from defeat in their personal, spiritual, and physical life. If there is any minuscule desire in you to leave your past behind and truly grab hold of who God made you to be before the shackles of life tie you down, then get ready to be inspired by Mike Whitfield's Rise and Hustle. Apply Mike's practical life changing advice and you won't recognize your life this time next year. You were made to thrive. To live abundantly beyond borders. Mike's book will show you daily habits, which will give you hope, and HOPE can resuscitate anything!"

— Rachel Best, Jesus lover, Homeschooling Mother
of Four, and Entrepreneur

"Mike Whitfield lives and breathes the Rise and Hustle movement. When we first met six years ago I knew he was going to make a huge impact on the world. Anyone who's been able to lose over 115 pounds and keep it off for years has an incredible amount of discipline and commitment. In his latest masterpiece, Mike gives an easy to follow blueprint tackling the major areas in life: physical, personal, and spiritual. You'll laugh, cry, and question what you've been practicing your entire life. If you're serious about living a life of purpose, passion, and commitment to excellence, this is a must read."

— Daniel Woodrum, Director of Turbulence Training

"Thank you for your thought provoking daily perspectives in *Rise and Hustle*. Life can get so complicated with all the noise and busyness; I love the simple "mini bites" of advice that Mike provides. His words have a way of simplifying things so that when applied, I can see the bigger picture. I can appreciate and live life more fully by reflecting on the simple premises that he brings up. Pure gold Mike; thank you again."

— Shawna Kaminski, Two-Time "Toughest Calgarian Alive"
Winner and CEO of My Bikini Belly

"*Rise and Hustle*. What a perfect title to devotionals that have motivated me to be more like Christ. Reading through these devotionals makes me see, as you have made very clear, that in order to "rise and hustle," we need to begin each day by giving it to God and use His example of "hustling" in our own lives. What a difference a 90-second read can do. Mike, you've been a true inspiration to me with how you have allowed

God to take control of your life and let Him direct your path. I pray these words will be an inspiration to many."

— Chanel Rivera, Sunday School Teacher and Deacon
at First Baptist Woodstock, GA

"Mike Whitfield overcame adversity and has gone on to achieve huge success through the practice of daily discipline; all with a heart of gratitude. Allow yourself to be moved by the sincerity and inspiration in his debut book, *Rise and Hustle*. This book is a must read!"

— Diana Keuilian, author of *The Recipe Hacker*

"The path to success is filled with deep struggles and huge defeats. There are moments when you simply want to lay down and give up. The stories that Mike has woven into the fabric of his new book, *Rise and Hustle*, have the power to lift you at your darkest hours and renew your spirit to press on and fight."

— Todd Kuslikis, CEO & Co-Founder of RallyAll.com

"I receive so many manuscripts to review for our Bookworm section; many I start, and quickly put down, but this one… I finished reading in one day. I truly could not put it down; I even began to use its quotes and began change in my personal and business life. What's next? I can't wait to actually read the book, one day at a time, and look forward to living the Rise and Hustle Lifestyle. If *Rise and Hustle* made an impact in one day, I can't imagine what it will do when I read each day and practice what I learn, *daily*."

— Mia Guerra, Executive Editor, *Chispa Magazine*

RISE + HUSTLE

NASHVILLE

NEW YORK • MELBOURNE • VANCOUVER

RISE + HUSTLE
Transform Your Life Physically, Personally, and Spiritually in Just 90 Seconds a Day

Published in New York, New York, by Morgan James Publishing. Morgan James is a trademark of Morgan James, LLC. www.MorganJamesPublishing.com

The Morgan James Speakers Group can bring authors to your live event. For more information or to book an event visit The Morgan James Speakers Group at www.TheMorganJamesSpeakersGroup.com.

9781683501817   paperback
9781683501824   eBook
9781683501831   hardcover

Library of Congress Control Number: 2016913586

Edited by:
Mavian Arocha-Rowe

Cover Design by:
John Weber
www.JWeberCreative.com

Interior Design by:
Brittany Bondar

In an effort to support local communities, raise awareness and funds, Morgan James Publishing donates a percentage of all book sales for the life of each book to Habitat for Humanity Peninsula and Greater Williamsburg.

Get involved today! Visit
www.MorganJamesBuilds.com

Dedication

I'd like to thank my parents for their ongoing support whether it was taking me to band competitions, encouraging me with this book, and everything in between. I'd like to especially thank my Dad for teaching me the entrepreneurial spirit. My Mom, who fights a disease called, "Myasthenia Gravis," and through it, has taught me the true meaning of perseverance.

I want to thank my wife, Sabrina, who inspires me every day with her outpouring of love to our two young boys, as well as being a rock for our family. Without her, this book wouldn't be possible. She is always in my corner, allowing me to chase after my dreams.

Finally, but certainly not least, I want to thank my CEO, God. I thought He was crazy for pausing my online business so I could write this book. But, as always, He has bigger plans than I could ever imagine.

Let Me Ask You Something...

How would you rate your physical health, on a scale of 1-10, with 10 being the healthiest you've ever been?

What about your relationships and family? How would you rate them? Are they getting your best or perhaps a fatigued and irritable "end of the day" version?

Do you feel like you're spinning your wheels, kind of "floating by" with your life? You're busy, yet you're not really getting anything done?

How about your spiritual walk? Is your relationship with God really thriving so you can benefit from His amazing grace and discover *your* purpose?

Indeed, there are thousands of books to improve each of the most important areas of your life—physical, personal, and spiritual. The thing is; you don't have that kind of time, do you? That's where *this* book comes in. In just 90 seconds a day, six days a week, you'll start transforming *your* life physically, personally, and spiritually.

A combination of humor, insight, admirable quotes, productivity hacks, and scripture await you. Each daily reading is short, punchy, and gets the point across to challenge your mind.

Yes. This is your time, and you will transform your life in just 90 seconds (or less) a day!

How to Use This Book

I hope you enjoy reading your daily "Rise and Hustle" as much as I enjoyed writing it.

The idea is to read one entry in the morning once you rise, and before starting the "hustle" of your day (hence the name, "Rise and Hustle"). We will focus on the three most important areas of your life:

1. *Physical*
2. *Personal*
3. *Spiritual*

Without a doubt, it's more challenging to improve one area without improving the others, however, they collaborate with each other. By improving in all three of these crucial areas, you'll discover more freedom, energy, and a sense of purpose.

Ready for your Game Plan?

Mondays — Physical Transformation
Tuesdays — Personal Transformation
Wednesdays — Spiritual Transformation
Thursdays — Physical Transformation
Fridays — Personal Transformation
Saturdays — Spiritual Transformation
Sundays — Rise and Hustle Sabbath: Consider this your day off and reflect back on the previous week, or use this day to catch up on any day you've missed.

The goal of every entry is to challenge your thoughts and actions. You will be given actionable insight in all three areas twice a week, and each entry takes 90 seconds (or less) to read.

Can you imagine the impact this can have in your life? Everyone in the world must rise, but only a select few choose to hustle. And since you're reading this, you've already made a wise decision.

But first...

Who Am I and Why Should You Listen to Me?

Sure, I've presented to hundreds of fitness professionals from all over the world showing my transformation strategies and I was a contributor to the *Men's Health Big Book of Getting Abs*. And yes, I did lose 115 pounds and have kept off the weight for 13 years at the time of writing this.

And yes, I did build an online business from scratch. And within a six months, I was able to quit my gym management job and cut loose of all my personal training clients thanks to the income from my internet business. More importantly, just a couple of months later, I was able to give my wife the ultimate job: being a stay-at-home-Mom who invests her heart and love into our two young boys every day. It's the most rewarding, yet hardest job any mother could have, but it was what we desired. And, this was something we thought, at one time, would be impossible.

Now, although my wife and I pray every morning with each other and we're the strongest we've ever been in our 10-1/2 year marriage, I need to be transparent with you about a few things [before you start on your journey with this book].

- I used to eat an iced honeybun and drink a Mr. Pibb for breakfast. I still get CRAZY cravings, too. I miss workouts and I still goof up with my diet.

- I've been divorced. It was one of the darkest moments of my life and I yelled at God for it. I lost my voice screaming in frustration.

- When I was working my corporate job, I felt like I was wasting space here on Earth. I was too blind to see any purpose.

This all changed when I decided to #riseandhustle. And, things are about to change for you, too.

I look forward to hearing about your success with choosing to #RiseandHustle,

 —*Mike (AKA "Mikey") Whitfield*

Things may come to those who wait,
but only the things left by those who hustle.
—*Abraham Lincoln*

Just Two More!

A few years ago, I had a client perform an exercise called the Goblet Squat. This is when you hold the end of a dumbbell and keep it against your chest, while you squat down and come back up. This exercise works your legs and abs at the same time.

I knew it was time to increase the resistance. She had been using a 20-pound dumbbell and I wanted her to try lifting 25 pounds. When I explained this to her, she gave me the same look I get from my wife when I tell a bad *Dad joke* like this: "The doctor just diagnosed me as being colorblind, Babe. I couldn't believe it. This really came out of the purple."

It was the same result, too—nothing could be heard, but the sound of crickets.

Then my client affirmatively said, "I haven't done anything that heavy yet; I'm not ready for this."

So, I *tricked* her like I have dozens of times. I went back to the dumbbell rack and pretended to switch them. Then, I gave her the heavier dumbbell. She knocked out twelve reps [she had been doing ten reps with a 20-pound dumbbell].

"Nice work," I said. "You not only crushed a heavier weight, but you also did two more reps."

She smiled. It was a smile that said: "I've been drinking the poison called *doubt* and I think I just purged it." What an awesome feeling.

This week, purge your poison. Rise, hustle, and defeat doubt by challenging yourself.

This Invention Destroys Your Dreams

The alarm goes off. You're awake. You have two choices:

1. Hit the snooze button and just lay there for nine minutes (because you and I both know you can't fall into a deep sleep in just nine minutes)
2. Get up, and win your morning

Nine minutes may not sound like a big deal, but look at the math:

9 Minutes X 5 Days per Week = 45 Minutes a Week

Now imagine, *not* hitting the snooze button and setting your alarm six minutes sooner. That's 15 minutes per day; 75 minutes a week, Monday through Friday.

Fifteen minutes, especially in the mornings, before the world smothers you with distractions, can be the difference between dreams achieved and dreams— well, just *dreamed.*

You snooze, you lose.

Starting tomorrow, stop hitting the snooze button. Move your clock or phone across the room if you have to. Win your mornings—and win your day.

That's how you rise and hustle.

He Is Relentlessly Pursuing You

In 1989, Armenia experienced a devastating earthquake. A father raced to the school that was all rubble; it was where his six-year-old son, Armand, attended. Even though there was nothing, but debris, the father frantically began digging to find his son.

He worked quickly, cutting his hands on the wreckage of bricks and rocks. Blood trickling, he continued to work. People tried to stop him, telling him that his efforts would not save his son. "Join me or leave me alone," the father replied; for 47 hours.

Forty-seven hours turned into four days. He was relentless and would not give up on finding his son. Suddenly, he heard an amazing sound: "Daddy, is that you?" Beneath the pile of rubble that was once a school, he finally reached his son, along with his son's classmates.

When his father pulled away the final bits of debris, rocks, and bricks to break free the children, Armand's face was glowing. Armand was safe. He told his classmates, "Didn't I tell you? I told you my Daddy would come. I told you my Daddy would come."

Maybe you find yourself under some wreckage of life. Perhaps the rubble of stress and discouragement has covered you. God is relentlessly pursuing you.

He can clear away the wreckage and rubble from your life. Just like Armand, you may not see Him removing the wreckage. Yet, he's working. Suddenly, you'll see His Hand reaching down to you, saying: "I told you I would come. I told you I would come."

> **See how very much our Father loves us, for he calls us**
> **his children, and that is what we are!**
> —1 JOHN 3:1 (NLT)

God is rising and hustling after you.

Why Should You Embrace Your Struggle?

Ever notice how we now live in a society of now, now, now? When we tap on the Facebook App on our phones, we expect to be on Facebook-*landia* in less than two seconds. If not, we have a tizzy. You turn on the hot water in your faucet; you expect hot water within five seconds. If not, you think something is wrong with your plumbing. You want to revisit the recipe from that delicious peanut butter cake on Pinterest, from your laptop. You go there and see the words: Internet Not Connected. Then you realize you're home alone so you take your laptop out back and beat the tar out of it while listening to an old-school gangster-rap. Wait. That's just me.

The thing is—we expect the same results when we try to adopt a new, healthy lifestyle. You want to be leaner, more energetic, and happier, *now*. Let me ask you this: *How can you enjoy the amazing, climatic ending to a movie without seeing the journey from its beginning?*

It's impossible. Be patient. Your climatic ending of a new, healthy lifestyle is on the horizon. However, the credits can't roll without the struggle. That's what makes your movie so great. The struggle with the plateaus—the cravings—the struggle of saying, "No thank you," are all part of your movie. Don't reject it. Embrace it. That's what makes the new you even sweeter. You'll appreciate this new lifestyle even more; and even more importantly, you'll keep it!

> *It's supposed to be hard. If it wasn't hard, everyone would do it.*
> *The hard is what makes it great.*
> *—Jimmy Dugan from the movie, A League of Their Own*

Embrace the struggle. Embrace the hustle. Rise and hustle.

Start This New Tradition

Every year, my wife and I go out for fondue to celebrate our anniversary.

We stuff our faces with mountains of fattening cheese, followed by eating a miniature bakery of cheesecake, brownie bites, and Rice Krispy Treats all dipped in warm chocolate ecstasy.

You may think this is my favorite part of our date, but it isn't… Just before we eat, we exchange a one-page letter reflecting on the previous year. We're completely open, sharing our victories, and our struggles. We also share our excitement for what's in store for the year to come.

We keep our letters in a binder as a reminder of how far we have come. And yes, feel free to use this idea with your spouse.

> *Gratitude unlocks the fullness of life. It turns what we have into enough, and more. It turns denial into acceptance, chaos to order, confusion to clarity. It can turn a meal into a feast, a house into a home, a stranger into a friend. Gratitude makes sense of our past, brings peace for today and creates a vision for tomorrow. —Melody Beattie*

This is my challenge to you: Write a letter to yourself. Reflect back on your victories and your struggles. Share it with your spouse, family members, mentor or whomever you feel comfortable with.

Every year, you'll see how far you've come and get the inspiration you need to make next year even better.

And, that's how you'll rise and hustle into a new year, no matter what the calendar says.

Exercising Your Faith

To preserve and build muscle, you need to lift weights. For example, to make a Dumbbell Chest Press *effective*, you need to control its resistance. This exercise comes in handy to push a full grocery cart or even a heavy door. These things become easier to handle with the perseverance and repetition of exercise.

Similar to your physique's build, your faith is a muscle. Are you prepared to push away the resistance?

Resistance is everywhere.
It shows up when we don't get the promotion we thought we would get.
It shows up when bills keep piling up.
It shows up when a family member becomes very ill.
It shows up in a separation or thoughts of divorce.

Without faith, we end up consuming this resistance and we let it control us. We didn't prepare for these storms, so we don't have the strength to control them. Now if it were up to *you*, would you be willing to allow these storms to arrive? Of course not. So what is God trying to teach you in your storm?

Consider Him your trainer. He is giving you some exercise for your faith. He won't give you so much resistance that you can't handle it. *He knows your strength better than you do.* Faith is a muscle and it must be exercised. Without exercising it, you won't feel the joy of hope, and with that hope, comes victory.

> **In this you greatly rejoice, even though now for a little while, if necessary, you have been distressed by various trials, so that the proof of your faith, being more precious than gold which is perishable, even though tested by fire, may be found to result in praise and glory and honor at the revelation of Jesus Christ.**
> **—1 Peter 1:6-7 (NASB)**

Rise and hustle daily—*in faith.*

When Goal-Setting Doesn't Work

Goals. Everyone and their brother "preaches" how you must set goals in order to make progress. But, here's why goals are a horrible idea: you focus way too much on the outcome.

For example, you might want to lose 15 pounds. So there you go, put up a fancy Microsoft Word Doc on your wall with the Nike symbol that says: *Just Lose It.*

But, do you know the process to get there? You don't think an architect just "wings it" when a house is built, right?

Here's a *new* way to use goals that will completely change the game. It's called *Process Goals.* Instead of focusing on the outcome (weight loss), you will focus on the process (road map) to get there.

Again, let's say you do want to lose 15 pounds. Here's a couple of sample process goals you would use for the next four weeks:

1. Exercise three days a week for 30 minutes (which equals to 12 workouts)
2. One or two reward meals per week (that means a maximum of eight reward meals)

Here's the hard part: Don't worry about the outcome. Just focus on the process.

Create a detailed process goal-setting plan for the next four weeks. The bigger challenge? Don't focus on the outcome. In fact, *hide* your *scale, and let's see* what happens.

Enjoy the process to enjoy the outcome of your hustle.

The Device Detox

This was the biggest challenge I've done in months. It changed my perception of quality time forever.

This will challenge you, too, and only a few people can pull it off. This month, I pretty much *dare* you to try it: **Device Detox.**

Before this month is up, I *dare* you to go a full day without your phone, computer, or tablet. TV is okay, but it must be kept to a minimum.

I did this for the first time a few months ago and realized how addicted I was to working when I was supposed to be having family time.

It was embarrassing, but you know what? My family time has been *more* amazing since that day. Now, I aim to have a device-free day once a month. And on Sundays, I refuse to read emails.

Go ahead. I *dare* you.

Before the month is over, one *full* day without devices. You'll be surprised at how hard it is; yet invigorating. Calling a Device Detox for all: Rise and hustle.

Gratitude Attitude

My No. 1 priority happens first thing in the morning—this is the one thing I refuse to skip. My alarm goes off at 4 am for this very reason. It's been a life-changer for me. *It could change your life, too.*

I get my Gratitude Journal and write down three things that I'm thankful to God for. Then, I read a short devotional, along with more scripture, which I will share later. I finish by praying for whatever is on my heart. This completely transforms my mind and my attitude for the day. Reading this could be overwhelming, but I still encourage you to get started. I suggest starting with three minutes.

Get a plain notebook that you can buy at a supermarket for under $1. Write down three things you're grateful to God for. (This can be anything.) As an example: I've written down simple things like playing with my boys the night before, going out to dinner with my family, my health, my home, or a great workout.

After you write down your three things, pray that you face the day with a better attitude. Pretty simple, right? *You can do that.* Follow this for two weeks and build from there. It will be the best habit you've ever started.

Every good gift and every perfect gift is from above,
coming down from the Father of lights with whom there
is no variation or shadow due to change.
—JAMES 1:17 (ESV)

Be thankful and then start your day. Ready to rise and hustle?

The Same Mistakes Every Year

In an interview during a podcast, one of the questions I was asked was, "What's one of the mistakes you see from people who want to start a new diet or health regimen?" I'm *so* glad he asked. This especially happens in January, but any time of year, *really*. Why do people have this "Gung Ho" mentality where they either have to live and breathe diet and exercise, or completely abandon the idea of getting healthy? *Don't fall into this trap.*

There's a "happy medium" that is very doable. You're going to be tempted to "out-train" a poor diet and lack of exercise from months (or longer). You'll be tempted to hit the gym six days a week. You'll be tempted to drink protein shakes and eat chicken breasts 24/7. You'll be tempted to give yourself no wiggle room for error and when you do "mess up," you *may* want to beat yourself up.

It doesn't have to be this way. The real secret to feeling and looking your best is consistency. Show me a man or woman that exercises three days a week, eats more fruits and veggies, while "indulging" one-two times a week.

Then, show me a man or woman who dreads going to the gym for their sixth day in a row, who feels they are missing out on life because all they live and breathe is a boring diet.

After four weeks, you'll see that option one is vibrant and more energetic, who happens to be dressed in clothes that feels more loose.

The second option? Minimal progress, stressed out, and abandoning the entire idea after four weeks.

Be real. Commit, but *don't* destroy yourself.

Make small, incremental changes. These changes will build your success. They will build your hustle. Now rise and hustle.

No. 1 Time-Sucker of All Time

I have no choice but to be extremely productive. In other words, if I'm not productive, I would wither away. My business would die; gasping its last breath. You see, that's the secret to starting or advancing your own business. You don't have to work insane hours. You can do six hours of work in just two. Let me explain:

After working in the corporate world for years, and being an addict to this time-sucker, I learned a very tough lesson: *Email is the No. 1 Time-Sucker of all time.*

Do you want to have an unproductive day? Then let someone else's agenda in your inbox dictate what you do. You see, when I get up at 4 am every day, I don't go to my inbox. That would be a bad move. Why? I would see something I need to take care of and then neglect the important things. No way—I'm not doing that.

Instead, I write. I brainstorm. I take care of my readers. This is how I'm able to produce hours of work in just two hours. I don't even have my inbox open. Once I do my most important tasks, I'll check my email quickly, then again in the late afternoon. Yes. *You read correctly.* I visit my inbox twice a day. Not seven, 15 or 30 times a day.

And, this is why I've tripled my productivity over the years. It will triple your productivity, too. Who knows what can happen? I'm guessing very cool stuff like *spending more time with your family or friends, starting or advancing your own business, playing "BINGO" with Grandma, and creating memories.*

If you're an email addict, this can be your drug. So, "ween" yourself off. If you're checking ten times a day, try eight times a day for two days, then six times a day for two days, etc. Watch your productivity go through the roof. Just do it; it's like a Band-Aid. Rip it off, then rise, and hustle.

Do You Need Patience or Endurance?

Do you ever say, I wish I had more patience? In church, on Sunday, one of my friends in our Sunday School class brought up an interesting point: the difference between endurance and patience.

Is there a difference?

I used to not think so, but something inside made me think differently. If I prayed for patience with my two-year old, I'm admitting I don't like my perception. If I am annoyed or I'm frustrated, I need patience.

However, if I ask for more endurance, I'm asking to endure what I'm facing— not a way out.

Let's take running for example. If I hated running, I would ask for patience: Give me the patience to *just get through it.* But, if I loved running, I would ask for more endurance: Give me endurance so I can run more or be more efficient at my sport.

It's about perception.

I know my little boy will only be *this* way for a short while. I don't want to miss out just because I don't have the patience. No way. I want to have the *endurance* to enjoy it. You see, there *is* a difference.

If you have been praying for patience and your prayers haven't been answered, perhaps endurance is the answer?

> **Being strengthened with all power according to his glorious might**
> **so that you may have great endurance and patience.**
> —Colossians 1:11

I also bet if you improve your endurance, even during your trials, you would find yourself able to rise and hustle.

Your Worst Hidden Enemy

Your enemy is not carbs.

Nor is it gluten, a bad workout program, your genes, or a slow metabolism.

Instead, it's an enemy that will grow every minute of the day because you keep feeding it. The more you feed it, *the more it thrives* and robs you of doing your absolute best.

This little punk preys on way more than just your desire to get in shape. It can destroy your relationships and your business.

Its name is Doubt, and *this* punk is your *real* enemy.

Eliminate it now. You can kill him in an instant.

Prove him wrong with action. He hates that. He withers away. It destroys him.

But, be warned. He *thrives* on procrastination.

Whether your enemy takes over you or you kill him; that's up to you.

Take action or procrastinate—let the games begin. Now rise and hustle.

Your "Big Idea" Time

My mentor, Craig Ballantyne, has urged me to do this for a long time and my only regret is that I didn't start it sooner.

"Big Idea Time"

When you enjoy what you do, and you have big dreams, you tend to work, work, work. You refuse to hover around in Facebook-*landia*. You give up TV Shows. Your PlayStation gathers dust. In *Essentialism: The Disciplined Pursuit of Less,* I read about giving yourself time [each week] to creativity. My first instinct was: *I don't have time for this.*

I was wrong. You see, by giving myself 20-30 minutes every week where I don't have my phone or laptop—just a notepad and a pen—brand new, amazing ideas hit me out of nowhere. And, it translates into writing content, even faster.

Whether you have a dream of starting your own business improving your relationships, or a bucket list; add to it every week.

It's riveting. It's invigorating. It's inspiring.

I recommend you go to a coffee shop or a new environment. Then, spend 20-30 minutes writing down any ideas that come to mind; whether they're business-related or bucket-list friendly. This is one of the most powerful motivational tools you'll ever use.

Having one "Big Idea" day can push you toward *finally*. Rise and hustle.

Words

It was fun and scary. I'll never forget when I presented my first lesson to our Sunday School class as an assistant teacher.

It was on the book of James, Chapter three, verses 1-12. As I was studying for the lesson, something hit me: A simple rule I've never seen in the Bible.

We all stumble in many ways. Anyone who is never at fault in what they say is perfect, able to keep their whole body in check.
—JAMES 3:2

No way. All I have to do is watch my words and I'm perfect? *Sweet.* Hold on there, buttercup.

What words are you consuming through social media, TV, movies, and more? What words are going through your head when you're frustrated at something or someone? What words are you thinking when something doesn't go your way?

Then it was confirmed. This is much harder than it looks.

James 3:8 continues with **"…but no human being can tame the tongue. It is a restless evil, full of deadly poison."**

James, you got me brother. You should see the restless evil when I'm in traffic or behind someone slow on the road. I have some improving to do. But alas, I won't give up. I'll constantly strive to get better, and you will too. That's what we do. We rise and hustle.

Your Day One

The alarm went off. I rose, rubbed my eyes, got out of my warm bed, and got ready. I didn't know the temperature outside, other than it was a freezing, bitter cold.

I drove over to my old high school track. I parked the car and then thought: *This is it.*

It was 2003; I didn't I have an Iphone or Ipod. I had one of those "fancy" no-skip cd players designed for joggers.

Here I was; over 300 pounds, about to run a few laps. I had no idea what I was doing, but I had to do something.

My first lap was going to be a warm-up of just walking. I didn't realize the warm-up alone would almost crush me. After just a single lap, I was exhausted. Tears fell down my cheek.

Am I too late? Will I be able to do this? Doubt and fear captured my soul. I went ahead and powered through with determination.

I jogged a little; walked a lot. Jogged a little; walked a lot. Roughly twenty minutes later, I decided that was enough. That was Day One. I started—and that was the most important day of my entire journey.

Today, almost 13 years later, I am 115 pounds lighter, and in much better shape at age 41 than I was at 28. And, it all started because of Day One.

What about you? Have you tackled your Day One yet?

Rise and hustle for *Your* Day One.

Why Stress is Your Fault

My wife was in Haiti for one week on a mission trip. That meant I was in charge of our two young boys. I knew I *could* work during the day while I watched them. I could throw on some *Veggie Tales* or perhaps *Cars* (and have them see this for the 3,447th time; they may even have the credits memorized). *Then*, I could begin work on my laptop.

But months ago, I told myself this week was going to be all about *them*. I planned to start the day with quiet time, and then work on my business until they woke up. Then, once they were up, it would be 100 percent them.

Scientific Fact: They are only going to be this young *once*. To have this much time alone with my sons is a gift; not a curse. I tend to seize the opportunity.

Sure, I could have told myself I would get some work done while I watched them. But, then I began to imagine the stress of breaking up a fight between the boys during my creative-thinking-time. Hmm—they're fighting over the same blue train, although there is another one just like it sitting across the room begging to be played with. This stress would be my own fault.

Instead, I planned to rise early like I always do (at 4 am), enjoy some quiet time, and then work until the boys woke up. I was ready: The second they walk out of their bedroom door, all of my time will be dedicated to *them*.

I planned on not getting much done that week; and that was okay. My advice? Seize your moments. When it's time to be with family, *be present*. Don't just sit there. Plan on being with your family; nothing else.

If you try to do both, you'll fail. You'll also stress yourself out and that will be your fault. Sure, you must rise and hustle in your work. But, doesn't your family deserve some hustle, too?

Daily Thank You Journal Template

As I mentioned before, for years, I've been journaling consistently every morning. *If you want to change your life and your attitude drastically, start a daily gratitude journal—that's how powerful this can be.* You might be wondering where to start and that's okay. Use this template as an inspiration; I have broken it down by morning and night.

Morning

Write down three things you're thankful for:

What would make *today* great?

Daily Attitude Check:

I am _____ (something positive here)

Night (Optional)

Three amazing things that happened today:

How could I have made today better?

Quite frankly, we're spoiled. We have it great. Why wait for a yearly holiday to initiate thoughts of thanksgiving? There's so much to be thankful for and what we need is a constant reflection on our blessings.

> **In every way and everywhere we accept this with all gratitude.**
> —Acts 24:3 (ESV)

Certainly, you can find a way to get up five minutes earlier for an instant attitude adjustment; right? I know it will improve your ability to rise and hustle.

By the way, you can download the daily gratitude template here: **http://riseandhustle.com/resources/**.

The Worst Thing You Can Do

Comparing yourself with *anyone* but yourself is by far the worst thing you can do while trying to change your health. Don't do it. You'll drive yourself crazy—and perhaps—those around you too.

Other people *will* lose weight faster than you. Other people will do it easier than you. And yes, other people have better genes than you. We must accept this and move on.

The only person you should ever compare yourself with, is the person in the mirror.

Who cares what a celebrity is doing? Who cares what your friends are doing?Are you doing things better this week than last week? Then—keep going. *This* is what matters.

Stumble. Fall. But never, *ever* stop going.

It's you versus you. That's it.

Compete? Sure. Compare? Never.

However you can, always rise and hustle.

Instant Smile, Guarantee

I suggest you try this—at least once—it's one of my best stress remedies.

One day a week, "I meet the outdoors" or head to a local coffee shop with two *Thank You* cards at hand. I write a short thank-you-note to a peer in the fitness industry and a family member. Other times, my efforts are dedicated to a good friend that I'm thinking about.

My notes are not long-winded or filled with "sugar-coated" words. Instead, they're honest. There's nothing wrong with just saying, "Hey, I just wanted to say I appreciate you." And, I can be funny, too.

For example, I sent a thank you card to my parents for dealing with the younger version of me. As a kid, I used to be very slow at eating dinner, and now, I'm suffering through this with my son, Champ. Along with my note, I attached a photo of a brittle old man and next to the picture I wrote the words: Mikey, after Champ *finally* finished his dinner.

I know you're busy and you may not "have time" to do this kind of thing, but it can change your perception. *Actually, it really should be a part of your life.*

People love getting a personal letter in the mail. Email? Anyone can do that. Nothing beats the ink on a hand-written note, especially if it's a thank you card.

Show people you appreciate them. You'll re-energize yourself while putting a smile on their face.

It's just one *wise way* to rise and hustle.

Your Shelter During the Storm

I sat on the steps of my house looking out the window for hours. I couldn't quite understand what just happened. A divorce was on the horizon. Just like a summer thunderstorm, it came out of nowhere and it nearly crushed me. Just a few weeks later, my loyal dog "Leroy" died of old age (he was about 16). The bills were piling up, too. *I questioned whether I would survive or not.* But here I am, years later, happier than ever with a marriage of over 10 years and two young, amazing boys—and yes, with a dog and two cats. I bounced back from what was one of the worst life storms I've been through (along with my two-year old being very sick at seven weeks of age).

Perhaps you're in the middle of a storm yourself, questioning if you'll survive the winds blowing against you. *The question is: Where's your shelter?* Is it alcohol? Is it being negative to those around you? Is it being hateful to your family because it's only raining on you? Those shelters wear down. I suggest you go to the Shelter found in Psalm 91:1, which says: **"Whoever dwells in the shelter of the Most High will rest in the shadow of the Almighty."**

Why? Because this is what He can do:

> **A furious squall came up, and the waves broke over the boat, so that it was nearly swamped. Jesus was in the stern, sleeping on a cushion. The disciples woke him and said to him, "Teacher, don't you care if we drown?" He got up, rebuked the wind and said to the waves, "Quiet! Be still!" Then the wind died down and it was completely calm. He said to his disciples, "Why are you so afraid? Do you still have no faith?"**
> —LUKE 4:37-40

Who or what is your shelter? Rise and hustle through *your* storm.

Dealing with Decision Stress

It happens to the best of us: **Decision Stress.** *Should I eat this? Should I drink that? Can I "squeeze" in some exercise today?* Getting healthier shouldn't be stressful. It's supposed to do the opposite.

Ready to avoid Decision Stress?

Create simple rules that you will follow; no exceptions.

For example, here are a few of my wife's rules:

1. I will use resistance exercise three days a week to help me manage stress.
2. I will stay active by going running or going to a kickboxing class in the mornings twice a week to stay alert and feel young.
3. I will not drink soda of any kind including regular or diet soda. Instead, I will drink carbonated water such as seltzer because I know that soda is not good for my UC (Ulcerative Colitis).

See how this works? It sets her up for success. If my wife's friend asks her to go out during her exercise time, she doesn't stress about it. She simply responds with, "Sure, but it will have to be this afternoon," knowing she is committed to resistance training that morning. She gives herself ample time to get her exercise in and not stress. If she's offered a diet soda, she doesn't have the mantra "Should I or shouldn't I?" going through her head. She simply responds with, "No thank you." Her proactivity eliminates decision stress from her life.

Here's my challenge to you: Take 15-30 minutes sometime today and create your own **Health Rules**. Think of three, or even as many as 10, however, any more is overkill.

You'll soon discover it's much easier to make decisions because you have *your own rules* in place to guide you. Sometimes, you'll break your own rules. It happens. But, at least you have something in place. And, this makes it *much easier* to rise and hustle.

Self-Control

Do you ever wish you could be a lot more productive? I do—all the time. I've read books on productivity. It's universal law...

...the more productive you are, the more you get done. The more you get done, the closer you get to your goals. #Science

Yet, the irony is that some folks read books on productivity, yet hop on Facebook multiple times a day. Or, they check their email ten times a day. Or, every 30 minutes they check the latest news sites, including Drudge Report so they can educate themselves, also known as scare themselves—because, it's really productive. #Sarcasm

Big Idea: Simply do a Google search for apps that block sites on your computer. (I personally use "Self Control," but find one that is compatible for your device and your lifestyle.

You set the duration (90 minutes, for example). For those 90 minutes, you can block any digital interruptions found on websites, like your email or Facebook, etc. The cool part? There is *nothing* you can do. You're almost "forced" to get things done. Google it. Get it. Triple your productivity, and most of them are FREE.

Use it to get more done so you can spend time with your family and friends without the guilt—this is the true meaning of *Rise and Hustle.*

The Harsh Truth About Your Rush

It was 4:45 p.m., about 30 minutes later than my usual "end the workday" time. There I was, writing like I was possessed, trying to finish up another article that wasn't going to be seen for another three days, when my two-year-old [at the time] walks into my office and decides to yank several books off my bookshelf. For no reason; this is exactly what he did. Perhaps he knew I was working overtime? Who knows? Out of frustration, I yell: Seriously?! Needless to say, he was upset and quite frankly, I was more upset with myself.

This happens to the best of us. We try to squeeze more in, and it ends up overwhelming us.

...oh, just one more article and I'll be three days ahead!

...oh, just one more email and I'll be that much closer to having my inbox cleaned up

...oh, if I could just clean one more room, my house would be 100 percent clean and I won't have to deal with it tomorrow.

Our intentions are good, but our attitude turns sour. Thankfully, Psalms has some insight for us:

> **We are merely moving shadows, and all our busy rushing ends in nothing. We heap up wealth, not knowing who will spend it. And so, Lord, where do I put my hope? My only hope is in you.**
> —Psalm 39:6-7 (NLT)

The next time my son walks into my office and decides to explore, I'll cherish it because he won't be like this for long—and I will miss it. Stop the rush. Enjoy your family and friends, even when you rise and hustle, daily.

Kick Him Out of the House

I'm speaking from experience. You know that "willpower" you're supposedly trying to improve? Kick him out.

He's over-rated, sucks your energy, and doesn't make much of an impact on you.

For example: My wife got these dark-chocolate almonds from Trader Joe's. I can eat one and be satisfied (they are huge). But yet, they taste so good, I'll eat one... two... three...

...well, you get the picture.

I asked her to replace them with chocolate-covered cherries. Guess what? I hate cherries. I think they're gross. Now, I don't have to waste my energy trying to "fight" from eating those chocolate-covered almonds. They got kicked out.

Who do you have to kick out of your home today? Don't just read this. You *know* what to do.Rise. Hustle. Kick.

Time for a Reset

My one "mid-life" crisis gift is sitting upstairs in our home in a corner of the loft area. We purchased it almost a year ago.

It's a used drum set. Way, back in the day, I used to *jam* on the one that was in my high school band room. Since being a teenager, getting one for myself was a dream of mine.

One morning, as I was going into my son's room to say hello, I noticed a little dust on it. I shook my head. Has it been that long since I've played? Why? I *love* playing. "I don't have time" was my pitiful excuse.

And, that's why we live in a *rush-rush world*. It's a constant *go-go-go* without giving ourselves a chance to *reset*.

As a result, I'm going to fix that. I'm going to start scheduling time to do fun stuff with my family. My boys love it when I *jam*—they even dance. That dust is going to come off the drum set and the drum sticks will come alive.

Now it's *your* turn. What's the *one* hobby you haven't done in a while because you *don't have time*?

> *If you're in a car and freaking out about how fast you're going, do you step on the gas pedal? Of course not. So if you're freaking out about how fast life is going by, try slowing down.*
> *—Mike Whitfield*

Rise, hustle, and reset.

Found Guilty, But Proven Innocent

I was in a groove with my workday and my wife asked me if I could join her and our two boys at the park. We didn't plan on going, but she thought maybe I could join them. Unfortunately, I was in the middle of a project. I could have gone, but I knew the project would dominate my head and I really would not have been *present*.

Within minutes, the guilt crept in.

I'm not being a good father. I'm missing out on quality time. It looks like work is more important than family.

I ended up shaking my head and realized that feeling guilty was *my own* fault. You see, the enemy loves it when you feel guilty; especially if it's something you shouldn't feel guilty about. That guilt leads to being silent. That guilt eats at you, over and over. The next thing you know, you're absorbed in silence; you fail to move on, and the rest of the day becomes a "woe is me" period.

Plus, you experience spiritual inactivity, and that's when the Enemy has won. The good news is, you can avoid this. Simply stay connected to God through His Word, daily.

The godly may trip seven times, but they will get up again. But, one disaster is enough to overthrow the wicked... —Proverbs 24:16 (NLT)

Understand that you'll never be perfect. Also, understand the Enemy *loves* when you're feeling guilty; especially when your guilt is unnecessary.

> *What you believe is very powerful. If you have toxic emotions of fear, guilt and depression, it is because you have wrong thinking, and you have wrong thinking because of wrong believing. —Joseph Prince*

Rise and hustle; without the guilt.

Slooooooooooow Down

On the way home from San Diego one summer, I had a layover in Charlotte, North Carolina. Usually, my layover is an hour, but this time, it was over an hour and a half. My laptop's battery was dead from working on the plane; working was out. I treated myself to eating and people watching. People watching rocks [and you know it].

I had stir-fry grilled steak, broccoli, mushrooms, and brown rice (I had pancakes earlier that morning; I had to be somewhat good). I was given the option of a fork or chopsticks. I wasn't a chopstick master, so I decided with chopsticks since I had time to kill. The serving was perfect; it was filling, but not an overload. It took me around 20 minutes to finish my meal [because of the chopsticks], and this got me thinking: *Are chopsticks an untapped resource to help you eat less?* Then I thought: *Man, if this is all I can think of, I need to get a life.*

Regardless, the chopsticks slowed me down, and this is my odd advice to you, who desires to improve their health: Slow down.

I can bet money that if you slow down when you eat, you will feel better, look better, and perhaps even enjoy your food more.

Our culture's mentality is go-go-go, but when it's time to eat, stop and enjoy it. Let it be your reset button. For an accomplished rise and hustle, hit reset.

The Power of Habits

Habits are powerful. They can change your life and are *very* underestimated.

Unfortunately, the power of habit has diminished because we've shifted our mindset to "I need to do that," instead of actually *doing it*. My question for today: How do you make habits *stick*?

1. Start Conservative

Want to read more? Start by committing to 15 minutes a day; very doable. Going from zero reading to 90 minutes a day is quite a jump and this will overwhelm you. Start small. Build from there.

2. Commit to a Period of Two Weeks

If after two weeks the habit is a "pain," it's time to adjust. You don't fail because you change something, you fail when you quit.

3. Create a "Ritual"

Let's say you're trying to go to bed at the same time every night. Create a "routine" just before you go to sleep. Perhaps it's 15 minutes of reading with the TV off. Or, enjoy a hot tea.

Bonus Tip: Don't try too many habits at once. This becomes overwhelming and you'll lack focus.

Choose one or two habits to start weekly, and then decide it's time to rise and hustle.

How 2.3 Seconds Can Ruin Your Day

All it takes is 2.3 seconds... sometimes less.

It happens.

You're sitting in unexpected traffic...

Someone is in your way at the grocery store...

our computer is running slow...

Then you lose it. You yell.

You call the traffic light a moron.

our *inside voice* calls the old man who takes 15 minutes to figure out what kind of peanut butter he wants an idiot.

You slam your fist in defiance as your computer takes too long to bring up a website.

And just like that, your mood changes in less than 2.3 seconds. Your day is officially ruined—all because of a little *impatience*.

We were warned this would happen:

> **Those who guard their lips preserve their lives, but those who speak rashly will come to ruin.**
> —Proverbs 13:3

Don't ruin what could be an amazing day, and remember, it takes less than three seconds. Take a deep breath. Life is too short. There's no time for this kind negativity.

Instead, we need to spend our time on rising and hustling.

Enough is Enough

For crying out loud, you said, "This is the year I get in shape!" Yet, here you are talking about it. Enough is enough with the chatter. What a mess. First, go through your pantry. Any junk food? Any foods that you eat too much of because *they taste so good?*

Give that food to a shelter. Enough is enough.

How many times did you exercise last week?

If the answer is zero, then start exercising twice a week.

If the answer is one or two times, then make it three times a week.

If the answer is three or more; keep doing that.

Enough is enough.

Where do you go on Friday nights? Do you go to the so-called "Happy Hour" and whine about your job while eating monumental amounts of salsa and chips? Stop going. *Enough is enough.*

Confused on what to eat? *That's your fault.* You keep reading stuff about dieting. Quit reading stuff. You know what to eat by now; start eating more of the good stuff and less of the junk.

You're an adult now. You know what to eat. *Enough is enough.*

Forget the whole "this is the year" fluff. This is your *week*. *Enough is enough.* Start improving your health, *today*. Today, you rise and hustle!

Do You Need Help?
(Careful With Your Answer)

Do you need help with anything?

Now think a little bit before you answer that.

If you answer "no," your growth *will be limited*.

If you answer "yes," plan on *growing*.

You see; that's how it works. If you admit you need help, then you actually get it... you're going to blossom. If you're prideful and think you can do it all, in reality, you're limiting yourself.

I know I can only grow so much spiritually on my own. So, I'm a part of an online group with other men that check up on each other to ensure spiritual growth.

I know I can only grow my business so much on my own, which is why I get help from others when it comes to building my websites, customer service, and graphics.

You see, I've made that mistake of thinking "I can do it all" and instead, I limited my own growth. Are you making this mistake? If so, you should fix that ASAP.

The more you think you can do it without help, I *guarantee* the less you'll be able to rise and hustle.

Epiphany of the Year

I had an epiphany. We discovered that our four-year-old son, Champ, has Autistic tendencies. I'll admit, my first question to God was, "Why?" *Then suddenly; it hit me.*

You see, the last year or so, I've connected with Champ at a very deep level. There are some things that I can clearly communicate to Champ that my wife sometimes can't. Champ and I both like having things done a certain way. There are "rituals" we both like to do when we wake up, etc. If we are taken out of that ritual—well—we can get a little grumpy. And in high school, I was in the drum line, yet I couldn't read music. I would have my drum instructor play the piece and then I would immediately nail it, after a few tries.

I realized Champ's memory is really sharp on certain things. My memory is really sharp on certain things. Champ hates loud noises; he's sensitive toward this. I hate loud noises; I too am sensitive. And, I despise balloons. Perhaps I'm on the Autistic spectrum myself. I don't know, but what I do know is that God made me Champ's father for a reason. When he's scared, sometimes, only I can help him feel safe. When he's having an "off" day and no one else can relate, I can understand him. Perhaps this is why good things happen to good people like Champ. There's a bigger picture that we yet don't see, but God does.

"For my thoughts are not your thoughts, neither are your ways my ways," declares the LORD.
—Isaiah 55:8

It's not about why bad things happen to good people; it's about knowing that God has a plan for you and *you* just may not see it unfold, just yet. Hang in there. He's up to something. He's the master and He yearns for you to rise and hustle.

A Bad Year

In third grade, I joined a recreational basketball league. It was my first experience playing organized basketball. I remember being nervous, yet really excited. For me, this was the beginning of my love for the game, which impacts me to this day. After completing third grade, you would think that I wouldn't be playing these days. You see, although I loved the game, I went all year long without making a single basket until our team actually made it to the championship. *Then it happened...*

It was almost like slow motion. I still remember it like it was yesterday. My teammate passed me the ball as he was about to get double-teamed. I took one dribble, put the ball in the air, and BOOM, it went in! But, the bad news was that it didn't count. My teammate was fouled on his pass to me. So, not only did I not make a basket all year, but we also lost the championship. Basketball wasn't for me... right? *Wrong.* I play three times a week, in my 40s, with a bunch of guys in their 20s.

I see this similar mentality with people wanting to get in shape. They get their workout clothes. They get all excited about doing something new. They put in their hard work for one, two, even three weeks, but the journey doesn't add up to what they envisioned. They perhaps, *don't make a basket,* perhaps they don't lose any weight. So, they give up...

They shrug their shoulders and say, *"This isn't for me."* And, that's a shame because they're going to miss out on that first basket, that first pound coming off, those first pair of jeans in the next size down, that burst of energy. Is this you?

If so, keep playing. You're on the verge of *your* first basket. Just keep rising and hustling.

Six Reasons Why You May Give Up

1. You stop believing in yourself.

Think about it: when you started, you visualized your success, didn't you? Why don't you visualize anymore?

2. You allow the past to continue to haunt you.

After being with my high school sweetheart for 12 years, between dating and marriage, I became divorced. It crushed me. I didn't meet my wonderful wife of 10+ years until I let go of that hurt.

3. You give up your time.

Say "No" more often. It's really that simple. I recommend you read the book *Essentialism: The Disciplined Pursuit of Less* by Greg Mckeown.

4. You focus on your weaknesses versus your strengths.

You say, *you can't do everything*. I tried it, and failed. Until I got help, I didn't grow. Do what you love and *only* what you can do; get help for the rest.

5. You feel the world owes you something.

This may sting a little, but you don't deserve *anything*. I don't either. We have to work our butts off for it—that's the truth.

6. You may see failure as a sign to turn around.

NBA legend Michael Jordan missed over 9,000 shots in his career. Stephen King received 60 rejections before selling his first short story. Emily Blunt had a stuttering problem growing up, today she's a Golden Globe winner. These are people that *failed forward*.

How do you fix this? Do the opposite. Believe in yourself. Let go of the past. Be protective and smart with your time. Focus and leverage your strengths. Work your butt off and earn it. Fail forward. And of course, always remember to rise and hustle, *daily*.

How to Wait for the Storm to Pass Through

There was a nasty storm that came through our town of Canton, GA. The lightning scared both of our little boys and once the power went out, Champ decided enough was enough. It was roughly 2 am and he screamed. My wife darted upstairs to calm him down. Being 4 am at the time, I'm betting he felt like it took forever for his Mom, *his hero*, to show up.

You may remember: When you were a kid, time goes by so much slower. A "time out" of only five minutes felt like days.

But, what counts is that Mom came to Champ's rescue and in his mind, she was wearing a Super Woman cape and was *Super Mom*. Within minutes, the house was quiet again. Super Mom gave him a sigh of relief and comfort, and within minutes, Champ was sleeping peacefully again.

You know, we adults are a lot like this. We face a scary storm and we call out to God for help. We wait for what seems like forever. The *"Is he ever going to come?"* mentality invades our minds. Admit it: *We hate waiting.*

Our prayers are typically requests for God to hurry up and fix whatever it is we're going through instantly. The good news? You can trust His response, even if it doesn't happen in your time. Just like Super Mom, *He* is on his way.

I waited patiently for the Lord; he turned to me and heard my cry.
He lifted me out of the slimy pit, out of the mud and mire; he set
my feet on a rock and gave me a firm place to stand.
—Psalm 40:1-2

Of course, in this case, He's coming downstairs. You'll be rising and hustling, soon.

No. 1 Exercise for Losing Weight

I'm asked a lot about the best exercises for losing fat. I posted my answer on my Facebook page. It's not what you want to hear. Yet, the good news is, you won't break a sweat doing it.

You ready?

It's called the "No Thank You." I won't lie; it's harder than burpees, but this exercise is *way* more effective than thirty burpees in a row. I guarantee it.

For example:"Wanna go to Happy Hour and complain about our jobs while drinking ourselves silly?"

Say: *No thank you.*

"Wanna eat cake for the third day in a row because it's somebody's birthday, yet again, here at the office?"

Say: *No thank you, but happy birthday!"*

I know you just ate, but you must try a piece of my pie."

Say: *No thank you.*

Want to know my go-to "secret" when someone is persistent? I simply tell them I'm not hungry. It gets them off my back pretty quickly.

Try the "No Thank You" exercise a couple of times this week. Next thing you know, you'll find yourself in a groove.

Rising and hustling...

Your Three "Bottlenecks" With Three Solutions

1. Do you worry about the future or live in the past?

Thinking of past bad experiences hold you back, and worrying about the future will cause anxiety.

How to fix it? Keep a daily journal. Take three minutes to write what you're thankful for and anything in the future that you're excited about. If you want to reflect on something from the past, write down what you learned and be thankful that *it is indeed*, in the past.

2. Is your to-do list too long?

A few years ago, I would write my To-Do List of 15-20 things. Just looking at the list made me overwhelmed and anxious.

How to fix it? These days, I write down two or three things on my list and that's all I focus on. Don't live in your inbox, either. I check my inbox twice a day and only once on Saturday morning. If you spend two hours a day in your inbox, I *guarantee* you can spend just 20-30 minutes and still get your emails done.

3. Do you have no outlet?

Even if you love what you do for a living [like I do], you need an outlet. It's even more important if you don't enjoy what you do. If you don't have an outlet, you'll be bottled up with stress and no way to *decompress*.

How to fix it? An outlet is your escape. It's a place where you can relieve stress and enjoy yourself. If you're smart, you'll use several outlets. Mine include playing basketball, strength training, reading, and sometimes, although rarely, I play video games.

What do you enjoy? Do it more often.

If you don't, you'll be negative with your friends and family, and that's not productive nor fair to them.

Work on these; next thing you know, people will begin to see that you rise and hustle.

Strangest Marriage Ever

Imagine the day you marry your soulmate. It's a Saturday wedding at 2 pm. You have the time of your life. The "newness" of being connected at a deeper level is like an adrenaline rush. You celebrate into the night with your family and friends, and even dance the "Chicken Dance" as though no one were looking. Then the next morning, you wake up with your spouse. You can't seem to wipe the smile off your face. The connection is *real*. You then proceed to have a nice breakfast and conversation. You find out more about each other in this morning chat and you know there is still much to learn.

Yet, suddenly after about an hour, it stops. You choose to not visit with your spouse until the same day next week, for the same amount of time—roughly an hour. That would be the strangest marriage ever, *right?*

Indeed, and that's what we sometimes choose to do with our Savior, Jesus. We hang out for about an hour on Sundays, then we tell him, "We'll see you next week." How can you get to know someone that way? And, how can He open up the real desires of your heart when you only talk to Him once a week? He has so much more in store for you, but you have to give Him some quality time—much more than once a week, for an hour.

> **But seek first the kingdom of God and his righteousness,**
> **and all these things will be added to you.**
> —Matthew 6:33 (ESV)

Think about this. All it takes is just a few minutes each morning to rise and hustle.

Behold... The Paper Towel Roll

Back in the day when I trained more "one-on-one" with clients at a small family gym, a client would ask me something like, "Mikey, I've been doing this for two weeks and my spouse has yet to notice any changes. Why is that?"

And then, I would explain the "paper towel analogy" I learned from another coach.

Take a roll of paper towels.

If you take off the entire first layer, you won't see a difference in the size of the roll.

Take off two layers—you still won't see a difference.

Take off three layers—you still won't see a difference.

However, after taking off one layer at a time, consistently over time, you will eventually see a difference in the size of the roll.

That's how you should look at your own journey. Stay consistent. Keep chipping away, one layer at a time and you (as well as others), *will* see a difference.

You *must* keep rising and hustling.

Why You Should Be Selfish

If you're not being a little selfish, you're doing others a disservice. Let me explain...

I hit the gym two or three times a week. It gives me natural energy, clarity, and focus. This means, when I do other things, they will be done even better.

When I do things *better*, it gives my customers and readers more value. I read my emails, twice a day Monday through Friday, only once on Saturday morning, and *never* on Sundays. Time away from email helps me focus on improving my products and services. More importantly, it lets me give more quality time to my friends and family. The secret? "Batch" your emails. Read them all at one time instead of an email here and an email there.

And, if someone wants to "suck" my time, I have to say "No" sometimes.

How will you know if your time is being sucked?

Listen to your gut. Your gut is right.

For example, someone emailed asking me to look at their body wrap products to share with my fitness readers. I laughed and deleted the message. I didn't "act nice" and read their website on their product and give feedback. I was selfish. And, being selfish is going to help more people. As Larry Winget says, "It is possible to give so much of yourself away that you compromise the quality of what you have to give."

So go ahead, be a little selfish. Sometimes you have to be selfish in order to rise and hustle.

To Put It Bluntly...

In 2015, I learned that my softball coach from my teen years passed away. It was hard to imagine him gone. Whenever I think of him, I think of the young, fiery coach that bet me dinner that I wouldn't hit a home run against our team rival. To a 14-year old, this was more about pride than pizza.

As I came running around third base toward home plate, after crushing the ball, I pointed right at him. He stood there and smiled. He knew how to help push me, but more importantly, he encouraged me to do my best.

That was 30 years ago.

Now, he's in Heaven for eternity.

Just like that trip around the three bases with my "In the Park" home run, our time here on Earth is just a snippet compared to eternity.

Who are you encouraging?

Who are you helping?

My intentions are not to scare you, but yet I want you to pause and reflect on this thought. Your time here is very short. It really is just a second. And, you have no control over this matter.

Why, you do not even know what will happen tomorrow.
What is your life? You are a mist that appears for a little while
and then vanishes. —JAMES 4:14

Life is short isn't just a cliché; choose to rise and hustle.

This Drink Gets Hype (and It Should)

It's the one thing all the fitness gurus agree on, yet most people just have a "Meh" attitude with it.

It will improve your skin…

It will improve your digestion…

It will make you feel full; better than those appetite control pills…

It will give you more energy…

Now, you have to promise *not* to roll your eyes, Okay? Don't underestimate the power of this "power fluid." You ready? *Drink more water.*

Seriously—eliminate all the "noise" this week about your health and simply *drink more water.*

You don't have to be dramatic about it, either. Going from three glasses a day to 10 is overkill. Simply add two glasses of water a day, this week. Do this every day, then next week, go for an additional three glasses per day.

It's the world's most aggressive weight control; and it's pretty much free.

Don't dismiss this: You're not taking this seriously and that bothers me.

You know what? You'll probably find yourself sleeping better, too.

Imagine this: Drink more water so you can actually rise *and experience* the hustle.

Do This Twice a Day = Nine Times More Productive

Do you know what crushed my productivity in both the corporate world, and even when I became an entrepreneur? Emails.

I'd leave my email window open all day long. I would hear that "chime" and I would immediately go to my inbox to see what fire I needed to put out. The funny thing was, there were no fires.

Here's some truth:

> *Remember, the inbox is nothing but a convenient organizing system for other people's agendas. —Brendon Burchard*

If someone *really* needs you and it's an emergency, don't they already have your number? They can text you.

As for everyone else, follow this simple plan:

Step No. 1: Read and respond to your emails in the morning (*only* after you get more important stuff done).

Step No. 2: Read and respond to your emails at the end of your day. Otherwise, your inbox should *never* be opened. I learned this trick from one of my mentors Craig Ballantyne. This takes discipline, but you'll end up being nine times more productive.

You can't "rise and hustle" from your inbox.

The Problem with Dreaming

You've probably seen them all: *"Dream Big. Do Big Things"* and other cliché motivational sayings. We get pumped up and start working toward our dreams.

Did you know, it's okay to dream big about anything? The problem isn't that you dream *too* big—the problem is, you don't dream *big* enough.

You underestimate God's power.

Think about your biggest desires. *Who do you think put them there?*

When you depend on only yourself, sure, you can make progress. But many times, you'll end up frustrated and lost. Jesus explains why in the book of John:

I am the vine; you are the branches. If you remain in me and I in you, you will bear much fruit; apart from me you can do nothing.
—JOHN 15:5

Alright, grab your calculator. Let's do some math.

Dreaming without relying on God = Dreaming

Dreaming while relying on God = Dreaming *Big*

Now to him who is able to do immeasurably more than all we ask or imagine, according to his power that is at work within us.
—EPHESIANS 3:20

Or the "hip" way of saying it: "You ain't seen nothin' yet."

Rise and hustle—and rise and hustle *with* God.

Powerful Two-Word Sentence Helps You Lose Weight

"I'm full." This was my ticket so many times.

You see, back when I was trying to lose weight and worked in a corporate job, I would hang out with my co-workers. Occasionally, we would hit a bar on Friday nights. It was easy for me to skip the drinks [as I hate the taste of alcohol, except for Nyquil; indeed I am weird].

However, food was another challenge. "C'mon Mikey, enjoy yourself," they would say. Then I would explain how I was trying to lose weight and had to limit myself.

"Oh another few bites won't hurt."

Then, I got really smart and used the phrase: *I'm full.*

Suddenly, they would leave me alone.

Next time you're "trapped" and you're being pushed to get that extra slice of pizza or join in on the office birthday party cake, just tell them: *I'm full.*

Keep your momentum going as you rise and hustle.

Don't Think of the Purple Elephant

Right this second, do *not* think of a purple elephant.

Alright, fine. You actually thought of a purple elephant.

Well, at least don't think of a purple elephant fighting a leprechaun in a dual sword fight. Ahhh, see? Now you're thinking of a purple elephant fighting a leprechaun with swords—while smiling.

Guess what? The same thing happens when you talk to yourself.

"Don't mess up." Then, what happens? You mess up.

"I'm going to be so shy at my reunion and I bet I will come across as snobby." You know what happens? Indeed, you end up being quiet and probably looked snobby.

What you feed your thoughts is who you become.

Marinate on that for a bit.

Let it soak in.

Then, change your thoughts.

Instead of "Don't mess up," think "I'm going to dominate."

Instead of "I'm going to be shy," think, "I look forward to getting out of my comfort zone and re-connecting with some people."

And, quit thinking about that purple elephant [which you weren't thinking about until I just typed this].

Feed your thoughts right. That's how you rise and hustle, *better*.

And, You Thought It Wouldn't Happen

For a while, my wife thought we wouldn't be able to have children. After two years of trying, we had a boy and we named him Champ (how fitting, right?). Two years later, we had Deakan.

Meanwhile, a friend of ours at our church was determined to put together a mission trip to Haiti in hopes of building a school. She was well short on funds; they needed $10,000. She kept telling everyone that it would be alright.

It was.

She went to her mailbox one day and got a donation for her mission trip. You know how much it was? Yep. $10,000.

> **He said to them, "Because of your little faith. For truly, I say to you, if you have faith like a grain of mustard seed, you will say to this mountain, 'Move from here to there,' and it will move, and nothing will be impossible for you."**
> —Matthew 17:20 (ESV)

I'll just leave that there. It's up to you if you choose to believe—if you choose to continue praying—if you choose to rise and hustle.

You're Missing the Point

This works rarely, yet it's prevalent. You see your friends have photos of models and actors in their cubicle or on their mirror.

"I want to look like that," they say in their minds.

You see six-pack abs, chiseled arms, and a tushy you can bounce a quarter off of.Now if you want six-pack abs, that's fine. *I'm not here to change your mind.* What I do want, is to have you aim to achieve your own *celebrity status.*

People are focused on becoming someone else, rather than a better version of themselves.And with that, you're missing the point of starting any diet or exercise program.

Imagine yourself leaner, healthier, and with abundant energy as you look in the mirror every morning. This is *way* more powerful than any random celebrity that you'll ever meet. At least with the mirror, you'll see that reflection *every* day.

Have any photos of celebrities or models you're going after? How about taking those down and instead, create a better version of yourself—a "celebrity status" of your own.

This is a better way to rise and hustle...

Go, Go, Go

At age 14 in Rock Hill, South Carolina, I was one busy fella.

Let's see: I played in our church youth softball league as well as the children's league (the cut-off was 14 for children and youth started at 14; so I did both). I also played on the church basketball team. I attended church Sunday mornings, Sunday nights, and Wednesday nights. Monday nights were for basketball practice. Friday nights, I would go to the high school football game—small city, everyone went to this game. Saturdays were sport days filled with basketball and softball activities.

It was a constant go, go, go.

It's funny how you can handle that kind of lifestyle at age 14. But, once you become an adult, it's *just* too difficult to keep up with. *Yet, we're not willing to accept that.*

We try to have lunch with a friend, hit the grocery store with our children, run a few errands and then have dinner with our parents all in the same day.

We commit to three different projects, taking time away from our families all in the name of *busyness*. No wonder our first response when someone asks how we're doing is "Things are crazy!"

We make our lives *crazy*.

You do *know* you have the rest of your life, right? You don't have to accomplish it *all* in two day's time.

It's a little cliché, but really—stop and smell the roses, even while you're rising and hustling.

Too Many Mistakes

Perhaps you're in a job you hate because of poor choices on your career? Perhaps you're in a relationship that is strained beyond measure, and think there is no way out? Perhaps someone has put you in an unfair disadvantage—because you didn't want to take advantage of them? Oh, perhaps you haven't found your purpose yet. And, that's a big one that a lot of people, like yourself struggle with.

You might be questioning your self-worth. *I can understand that.* I've been there. You would do anything to see the light at the end of the tunnel, but you feel you have to "pay" for your mistakes first. Well, there is good news for you:

> **But he said to me, 'My grace is sufficient for you, for my power is made perfect in weakness.' Therefore I will boast all the more gladly about my weaknesses, so that Christ's power may rest on me.**
> —2 Corinthians 12:9

No friend, family member, or even your spouse can give you a sense of peace like God can.

He helps you forgive...

He lifts you up when you feel like lying down...

He gives you strength in your deepest moments of weakness...All you have to do is give him a call. His number is P-R-A-Y-E-R.

Give him a call. He's always there. He has a purpose for your rise and hustle, too.

They Are Watching You!

This will freak you out, but I learned this myself after losing 115 pounds.

People are watching you during your journey and you don't even know it.

They are seeing if your journey to better health is worth it. They are waiting to see if you fail or if you prevail.

And, you will fail. It happens to all of us.

Yet, this is the most critical part of your journey.

When you do fail, will you give up or keep going?

If you give up—well, you're going to let them down. It's like you're telling them, "It's just not worth it."

Yet if you keep going, you will give them hope.

Remember, someone in your *own* family may be watching you. They will never tell you, either. Deep inside, they want to make a change, too; they're just waiting to see if it's worth the effort.

Show them how to rise and hustle, *daily*.

Clean That Up

Clutter. It drives us all crazy. No matter how much counter space you have, it's all covered, *right*? You have mail, magazines, bills, recipes, dishes, and more covering every single inch. And, when you get more counter space, you'll cover that up, *too*.

When it's time to focus and do a little bill paying or perhaps cook dinner, it could be hard to concentrate. *I mean after all*, the pen is buried under the coupons, and the pan is buried under the dishcloths. One bill is under a stack of pans, while the other bill is buried under four issues of *Good Housekeeping*.

You give in. You clean up the countertops. The marvelous surface begins to reappear. Suddenly, you discover a whole new world. You find yourself standing in the middle of your kitchen, mesmerized by the clutter-free countertops, with your arms crossed, and smirk across your face. *Now*, you can cook like a boss, get the bills paid in minutes, and find yourself 10 times more productive.

How much more productive would it be to clear the clutter in your mind?

Are you putting so many things on your to-do list, that you find yourself spinning your wheels? Perhaps it's time to re-evaluate your list? Remove the things that are taking up space—much like the magazines on the countertop [that you're not going to read].

Ask yourself this question: Will your world carry on if your inbox isn't completely empty?

Clutter in your mind removes your ability to rise and hustle. Let's tidy up.

Take These Three Pills Every Day

Let me ask you a question: What kind of life would you experience if you:

1. Dramatically improved your attitude and outlook,
2. Experienced radical hope every single day, and
3. Overcame temptation victoriously with discipline.

These *three* things would dramatically improve your life. And, there are three pills you can take to experience all of this.

Pill No. 1 Attitude

Do not conform to the pattern of this world, but be transformed by the renewing of your mind. Then you will be able to test and approve what God's will is—his good, pleasing and perfect will. —Romans 12:2

Pill No. 2 Hope

"For I know the plans I have for you," declares the Lord, "plans to prosper you and not to harm you, plans to give you hope and a future." —Jeremiah 29:11

Pill No. 3 Discipline

No discipline seems pleasant at the time, but painful. Later on, however, it produces a harvest of righteousness and peace for those who have been trained by it. —Hebrews 12:11

Instructions: *Read* these three every morning with a cup of coffee and some quiet time.

Caution: *Do not* mix with life's distractions.

Discard By: Never. Take Every day.

Take these three pills daily—*that's* how you rise and hustle.

An Important Success FYI

This is what I call my **Success FYI**: Perhaps you have been comparing your success with what the world tells us. You know what? I did the same thing for a while.

So let me tell you something...

Success is not having six-pack abs, but it *is* having a core strong enough to crawl on the floor with your kids or grandkids so their laughter is smack in your ear.

Success is not having six percent body fat, but it is being healthy enough so you have more energy, drive, and focus during the day; with some energy left over for your family when you get home from work.

Success is not cranking out one 100 push-ups and posting it to Facebook, but it is about being just a tad better than last week.

Success is not being miserable, forcing yourself to eat kale and protein shakes 100 percent of the time. It is, however, finding that balance of fueling your life and enjoying a splurge now and then *without the shame.*

Success is not living in the gym, but it is being an example to others by taking care of yourself.

Success is not measured solely by the scale, but it is measured by being able to take the stairs [without hyperventilating].

To your *real-world* success... as you rise and hustle.

When Things Are Going Bad, Do *This*

When things are going bad and you find yourself banging your head against a wall, help someone else.

Bizarre, *I know*. But, it works.

For example, in my online business, if I am running a promo for a product that is not doing well and I can't figure out why, I just shrug my shoulders, stop, and help someone else with their promo.

They usually end up crushing theirs, and I am okay with that.

The next thing you know, you'll end up inspired or with an "a-ha" moment of how you can improve your own life and out of your rut... all because you helped them *first*.

We all have a little "rise and hustle" within us. *Sometimes*, we need a little push. This strategy is one of the most powerful and effective ways to do just that.

Help someone else rise and hustle.

Perception "Shift" Thanks to a Super Bowl?

It's funny how as you age, your perception changes. I've been a Carolina Panthers fan since they came into the NFL in 1995. In their first Super Bowl in 2004, they lost by a last minute field goal. I still remember my back being against my refrigerator as I slid down, with tears coming down my face. My old high school buddy reminded me of this moment when he came over to watch Super Bowl 50 between the Denver Broncos and Carolina Panthers. I don't mean to sound like a pathetic country song, but just before that Super Bowl in 2004, I lost my loyal dog to old age. And, I was also going through a divorce [I didn't want], and now my *beloved* team couldn't win the Super Bowl.

"If they only won, then my life wouldn't be so bad," ruminated through my head.

Boy, was I wrong.

Fast forward 12 years and my Panthers lose another painful Super Bowl. You would think another 12 loyal years would make the loss more painful. You know what though? It wasn't. Sure, I was bummed—I even had my pout face on. However, I have a wife that has been incredible to me for more than ten years, two amazing kids that have taught me more about life than I have taught them, and a "job" that effortlessly gets me up at 4 am [on weekdays] because I *dig* it so much. I don't need a Super Bowl win to validate if my life is good. *Sure*, it would be awesome and I hope my team has another chance at it. But, I have everything I need.

In 2004, I relied on a trophy. Today, I rely on His word.

And God is able to bless you abundantly, so that in all things at all times, having all that you need, you will abound in every good work.
—2 Corinthians 9:8

Perception—it's powerful, right? So when you're rising and hustling, remember what matters *most*.

Why Social Media is Not Motivational

On my Facebook page, I never share pics of women or men with six-pack abs with cheesy sayings like, "You Have to Want it Bad Enough!" or some other lame phrase. Frankly, this is why so many people are on edge. We're constantly pressured to look like someone you see on a cover of a magazine.

Then, we're supposed to feel guilt when we enjoy pizza on a random Thursday night, all because you saw a photo on Facebook of a skinny woman eating celery and the words: *Pizza Won't Give You Abs.*

This stuff doesn't inspire me, and I imagine it doesn't inspire you, *either.*

So instead of relying on social media for inspiration, *rely on yourself.*

Be proud of the moments when you make a great decision for your health. Then, enjoy your moments of breaking free from your regimen because you know you don't have to be perfect.

You can be *imperfect* and get healthy at the same time; *without the guilt.*

Rise and hustle; without the cheesy memes.

The Ugly Truth About Comparing Yourself with Other People

It's possibly the worst addiction you could ever have. It starts with just one little thing, but then it grows and grows. Minutes later, it overtakes your life...

It's called: comparing yourself to others.

This addiction will grow on you like a colony of E. Coli as though you were room temperature beef.

Stop comparing yourself to your friend that is thinner than you. Stop caring about someone else's bank account. Stop being so envious of someone else being more social than you.

In fact, quit worrying about what others think of you.

You're all tied up in someone else's highlight reel; you don't even know what's going on behind the scenes. Sadly, you're comparing their success with your struggle.

I've shared this quote before, but it's worth sharing again:

> *The reason we struggle with insecurity is because we compare our behind-the-scenes with everyone else's highlight reel. —Steve Furtick*

You know the ugly truth behind comparing yourself? *Being resentful for someone else's success is just another distraction that will slow down your own progress.*

Drops the mic, leave the stage, so you can properly rise and hustle.

He's Really Irritated, So Be Cautious

Have you ever noticed this in just about any sport: A team might be losing by a landslide and suddenly, they find this new *surge*? There's an *extremely* slim chance they could come back, but they scratch and claw their way trying to create a miracle. Then, the winning team almost gets too relaxed and out of nowhere, the losing team is back in the game. You see, the losing team is *irritated and frustrated*, so they start cranking it up a notch.

You know what?

The Enemy does the same thing.

Just when you think you're winning the game of life, the Enemy senses that and it irritates him. He can't stand to see you happy.

He wants you to doubt everything and stop leaning on God. When you're sad, the enemy is happy. *That's just the kind of jerk he is.*

As you get stronger with your walk with God, the enemy will try to pounce on you even harder.

You could say, "Well in that case, I might as well lay back then, right?" Nonsense. The stronger your walk with God, the stronger you'll be during dark times.

I'll take God on my side during my dark days [thanks to a strong relationship] over a laid-back "let the devil put all the doubt he wants into me" attitude, *any day.*

Be alert and of sober mind. Your enemy the devil prowls around like a roaring lion looking for someone to devour.
—1 Peter 5:8

Be strong, *and* cautious as you rise and hustle.

The Simple Answer to Why Change is Hard

Change is hard because people overestimate the value of what
they have—and underestimate the value of what they may gain
by giving that up.
—James Belasco and Ralph Stayer

Dieting stinks. *It is what it is*, right?

Taking time out of your week to exercise means you have to sacrifice something else like, TV time or perhaps less time with family.

Now, step back, breathe, and realize what you gain. *You will be surprised.*

Dieting is hard, but once you start eating better more consistently, how much *better* will your rewards taste?

A slice of cake every day won't taste nearly as good as it does once a week [especially when you've earned that one slice with a week of focused effort].

Indeed, being away from your family for 30 minutes a day, a few times a week doesn't sound appealing. Yet, when experiencing more energy becomes part of your day-to-day, what you share with them becomes priceless. The improved mood is pretty nice, too.

You might be surprised at how little you're giving up for the amazing things you gain. It's totally worth the rise and hustle.

Adopt This Immediately

I had to learn this the hard way and you need to adopt this as quickly as possible. The adoption process takes mere minutes and the best part—it costs nothing.

No lawyers. No courts. No approval process. You're automatically in.

Adopt a positive attitude. Now wait... *don't roll your eyes at me.* There's a difference between *working on your attitude* and *adopting a positive attitude.*

When you adopt, you're responsible for it. There's no turning back. You can't return it. That's how adoptions work.

Once you adopt a positive attitude, even when things are not going your way, you're ensured a positive outcome. I guarantee it.

That sounds bold, I know. But, a positive attitude means you'll have a positive perception. That means when things are bad, they become opportunities versus setbacks.

When you focus on setbacks, what happens to your progress? Exactly.

When you focus on opportunities, what happens to your progress? Exactly.

What will you do, now that you're done with the adoption process? Rise and hustle? *Exactly.*

The Best Time to Pray?

God's Word: Written by dozens of authors all having the same *theme*. Every single word inspired by Jesus and many verses spoken by Jesus, himself. There was a purpose for every word. It says so in 2 Timothy 3:16-17, **"All Scripture is God-breathed and is useful for teaching, rebuking, correcting and training in righteousness, so that the servant of God may be thoroughly equipped for every good work."**

Recently, I pointed this out in a Sunday School lesson. We were talking about the best time to pray. Now obviously, *any* time is the *best to pray*. But, if you truly desire to discover the purpose of your life, and experience hope and joy, daily quiet time is your *secret sauce*.

But when? The middle of the day? The end of your day? The beginning? Just before you go to sleep? The answer is clear. Raise your hand if you want to be more like Jesus. I'm guessing you're raising your hand—at least in your mind. *Great!* In Mark 1:35 we find when Jesus himself prayed, **"Very early in the morning, while it was still dark, Jesus got up, left the house and went off to a solitary place, where he prayed."**

This verse could have easily left out "very early in the morning, while it was still dark." But, God inspires every word in the Bible and every word has a purpose. He craves to hear from you first thing in the morning before the *busyness* of life distracts you from talking to Him. And, when you go to Him early, the Enemy doesn't have a chance to get to you first. That's some insight on how to start your daily rise and hustle.

Socrates? You Are Correct

When I worked at my corporate office job, the first year of my 115-pound weight loss journey was tough—I won't lie. Every Thursday, we had our weekly meeting and there they were—fresh bagels with an array of cream cheeses to choose from. Mmm; we're talking cinnamon bagels with a walnut chunk spread. Then, there's the classic cheddar cheese bagel with regular cream cheese. Between 400-600 calories of glorious gluten, baby.

It was an epic battle of will for me. Half the time I folded and caved. The other half, I stood firm, but walked out of the meeting exhausted [because I drained my willpower for the day]. Yes, bagels rock.

Have a good day. Rise and hustle.

On a serious note, I did this completely *wrong* for the first three months or so. You see, every Thursday morning just before the meeting, I started to dread using up all of my willpower. Instead, I could have used Socrates's advice, "The secret of change is to focus all of your energy, not on the fighting the old, but on building the new."

So, instead of focusing on the bagels I shouldn't eat, I got excited about starting new habits that would make my life easier.

Thirty minutes before my weekly meeting, I would make myself a small bowl of oatmeal; and added a teaspoon of peanut butter. I then showed up to the meeting feeling *satisfied*. Saying "no thank you" to the bagels was a walk in the park, and left the meetings without feeling sleepy [thanks to the carb coma].

Imagine putting this to work in all areas of your life, including your health? It makes this whole "I need to get in shape" thing a little easier and tolerable, huh? *Well played Socrates, well played.* I am certain Socrates rose and hustled using this strategy; why can't you?

Your Smile Could Be 24 Hours Wide

It was the fall of 2003. I was still working my corporate job and ended a long, stressful day. I walked down to the office gym, changed my clothes, and then headed toward the workout area. No one knew just how stressful my day was. I was [and still am] an introvert.

To add *more* stress, I was going through a divorce. I wasn't sure if I would sell my house. I wasn't even sure where my life was going. Quite frankly, I didn't find any purpose. So, I walked with a fake smile, as I roamed around the gym diligently doing my workout. I was smiling on the outside, but battling tears on the inside.

Then a woman, who I had never seen before, looked at me with a really large grin on her face and said, "You are working so hard! Keep up the good work!"

Swagger. Suddenly, I had *tons* of swagger.

I lifted weights like a boss. I ran on the treadmill like I was an Olympian with three percent body fat. I was pretending to train for the Boston Marathon; *and I hated running.*

I was on a "bliss" for the next 24 hours with my mood enjoying a 24-hour transformation. That's the power of a smile, with the bonus of a little encouragement.

You don't know what those around you are going through. Show them your smile. Shower them with kindness. Your two-second smile can last 24 hours, or more.

That's time well invested. In fact, your smile could help them rise and hustle.

Unwavering Belief

Have you ever been *so* high up, you kept telling yourself, *don't look down, don't look down*? Then what happens? Yep, you look down.

The same thing happens with your beliefs. If you're thinking negative thoughts, what happens? Yep, negative things.

When God himself reveals something good in your life—that you think is impossible, or "too good to be true," and you decide *it won't happen*—you're missing out.

Nothing is impossible with God.

He can miraculously give life when death is knocking on the door.

He can give birth, when you have been told you'll never be able to have children.

He can resurrect a bad relationship. After all, He Himself resurrected from death.

But, you have to hold your end of the bargain. It's called: Unwavering belief.

Trust in the Lord and do good; dwell in the land and enjoy safe pasture. Take delight in the Lord, and he will give you the desires of your heart.
—Psalm 37:3-4

Rise and hustle; with unwavering belief.

The Alphabet of Your Physical Transformation

Let me tell you a little dirty secret. Whenever someone sees my before and after pictures in my marketing campaigns, they sometimes ask what I did to make a difference. They don't see the struggle I went through. They don't see the low-carb diet I tried and failed miserably at—binging on nachos just three days into it. They didn't see the "cleanse" I tried, and bailed on, because it was just too hard for me.

It's not that I don't want to share these struggles (after all, I'm sharing them now). There is only so much time; so I share the *highlights* to inspire them into action.

Perhaps you've started a new exercise and diet regimen. You possibly have your workout clothes laid out nice and neat, on the edge of your dresser, every night. And, you may have your menu planned for the week. *You are ready to ROCK.*

Then, two weeks go by and your pants feel tighter as you stare at the scale with frustration. Remember this, you only discovered something that might not work for you. Please, stay cool.

Just because Plan A didn't work, there are still 25 more letters in the alphabet.

To *truly* rise and hustle, you must be willing to try Plans B, C, D, and more until you find your groove.

And yes, you *will* find your groove. Keep up your hustle.

Why Reading Books Doesn't Do Any Good

I'm a natural introvert. Give me a Friday night with the fireplace and a good book over a big party. I'm sort of a bookworm. Now, before you think I'm going to suggest the whole "The more you read, the more successful you'll become," stuff, hear me out. I'm about to do the opposite.

We live in a world of info-overload. Absorb, absorb, absorb is being crammed down our throats on a daily basis. After all, what's the point of reading and reading... and reading... and reading without actually applying anything you have learned because you're just, *overwhelmed?* You're not giving yourself enough time to process it. This when reading books for self-improvement doesn't do *any good.* Here's my trick to reading more and actually applying the info:

Step No. 1 Choose one personal development/spiritual development book.
Step No. 2 Read one or two chapters *only* in a day. No more.
Step No. 3 Over the next 24-48 hours, let it *simmer* in your mind. Ask yourself: How you I apply what I just read onto my life, or how can I be more conscious of it?
Step No. 4 Once you figure out how to apply it to your life, then move onto the next chapter, and repeat.

Why? Because reading without application is a waste of your time. *There; I said it.*

That doesn't mean you get to stare at a TV the rest of the time. You don't get off that easy. Go with fiction. It's a great way to turn off your brain and stimulate your imagination. I have what I call my "TV Book." I'll read a chapter of my personal/spiritual development book, and then dive into my "TV Book." Why this name? We disconnected our cable; *best decision ever.* It fueled reading, therefore fueling my imagination, and my personal and spiritual development. That's how to make books worth your time. Book it. Then rise and hustle.

When Prayer Doesn't Work

Years ago, I worked in the print advertising department for a large corporation. I'll be blunt: Trying to get the Merchandise Buyers to approve an ad was a frustrating experience. As an ad department, we *knew* what would look good in a magazine or flyer. However, the buyers always had their say-so and hardly approved an ad unless we changed it to their liking. The buyers didn't want to stick to what they knew. *They thought they were ad specialists, too.* So, we changed the process. We began to ask approval on concept versus final design. This made things work faster toward the approval process, and made our lives a lot easier. We got a lot less "no's" this way.

Unfortunately, we do the same thing to our Savior, don't we?

There's a difference between these buyers and our Savior. The buyers don't see the big picture, but our Savior does. That's why we make more work for ourselves when we put a plan into place *first*, then seek God for a "yes." We think by mapping out our plan, He'll respond with a simple "sure." However, His answer may be "no" or "not now."

A while ago, I was offered a promotion at a corporation. Something told me [perhaps *God*], that I shouldn't take this promotion. More money would have been nice at that time, however, just when I thought I would be stuck at my current job, my Dad reached out and offered me work. This opportunity allowed me to work side-by-side with my Dad *for a few years*, before starting my own business. I will forever cherish those memories of eating lunch with my parents and getting to know my Dad more. He also taught me the entrepreneurial spirit. Sometimes, you just don't see what God is up to. But, *He's always up to something.*

I will instruct you and teach you in the way you should go; I will counsel you with my loving eye on you. —Psalm 32:8

Rise and hustle in His way.

Oh No! Not Now; You're So Close!

Let me tell you about the mysterious "whoosh" effect. I learned this term from my friend and mentor, Craig Ballantyne. This effect happens when you're grinding it out, doing all the right things, yet you're not seeing a difference in your clothes or in the mirror.

Right at *this moment*, 98 percent of people quit.

It's just before that "whoosh" kicks in, *which is a shame*. The "whoosh" is when suddenly, you find yourself one or two pounds lighter or you finally see a difference in the mirror.

Weeks and weeks of frustration, then *bam*! It happens.

I've seen this happen in my journey, and in thousands of other men and women I've worked with, either in person or online.

Fair warning though: The "whoosh" *only* happens to those that hustle. The "dabblers" that try a new diet here and there, or exercise only when they feel like it, never get to experience the "whoosh" effect.

Don't stop now. You're so close.

> *Many of life's failures are people who did not realize how close they were to success when they gave up. —Thomas Edison*

Don't be one of the 98 percent.

The Top Two Percent never quit. They live the mantra of "rise and hustle"...

...and *whoosh*.

Does Anyone Hear You?

I've shared things through social media that I thought were amazing, yet no one really said anything about getting something out of it.

I've also promoted a product that I thought my readers wanted, but it ended up being a waste of my time. It was almost like saying, "Hey, does anybody want to buy this?" and suddenly you hear a crow "caw-caw" while a big piece of tumbleweed rolls by.

This happened to me a lot. And, it's going to happen to you, too.

You might be thinking, "Does anyone hear me?" with frustration.

Then, right when you're about to give up, you'll get that reply from someone out of nowhere on how you're helping them—all because of your unique voice, and the unique way you present your own insight.

For example, there are thousands of other "gurus" telling you how to be productive. Yet, I've followed my mentor and friend Craig Ballantyne for years because I simply resonate with him.

You're going to have followers like that, too. Whether it's in your business, in your church, or just hanging out with your friends; people are looking up to you, even if you think you're just talking to tumbleweeds.

Keep adding value to people's lives. Keep being open and honest. Share your struggles. Share your victories. They hear you.

And because of you, they are rising and hustling.

The "Presents" of Friends

I have a good friend named Tom that lives in Chicago. When he lived here in Georgia, he helped me get through some dark times, including a divorce and my physical transformation. I'll never forget after a workout in our first week, he said "Mikey, you are burning fat so fast there is fat on the streets!" In a weird way, that was very encouraging. I was fairly new to working out, so he gladly showed me the ropes and got me in the right direction. More importantly, his encouragement meant a lot to me.

Then there is Dan and Amanda, a couple I've known for about 20 years. When I told them about my surprise divorce, they were at my front door within two hours with some fresh hot wings, ready to watch NFL football with me. By the way, Amanda *hates* football, but that's the kind of people they are; ready and willing to sacrifice for me.

Looking back, I'm glad I wasn't stubborn and tried to get through these dark times on my own. Frankly, I wouldn't have made it. One day, during my divorce, Tom said, "We need to let Mikey get through this and let him feel what he's supposed to feel. But then, there will be times when we have to make Mikey get up and do stuff." That was priceless advice. I still thank Tom for that to this day. *Who has God put into your life that you're denying you need (when you really indeed need them)?*

God *does not* want you to go through life alone. Let your friends come over. Let them encourage you. Let them support you during your dark times. This is how it is meant to be.

> **Two are better than one, because they have a good return for their labor: If either of them falls down, one can help the other up. But pity anyone who falls and has no one to help them up.**
> —Ecclesiastes 4:9-10

Just because you rise and hustle, doesn't mean you have to rise and hustle alone.

Sorry, It's Not Enough

You have your MC Hammer songs on your playlist, right? Check. You went to Target and got those brand new workout shirts and shorts. Black and blue? Cool color combo. Check. Excellent choice on the new shoes, too. They are comfy and are ready to be broken into, right? Check. Now you're rocking two or three days a week of exercise in the gym or even in the laundry room at your house. Why the laundry room? Well, *why not?*

You're rocking with your chicken breasts and green beans at work five days a week. Excellent!

So with everything in order, you should be dropping pounds like a boss, right?

Well, the truth is, it *may not* be enough.

You have the big picture taken care of, but if you're still struggling, it's time to look at the smaller things. The small things can make a big difference. Will simply drinking more water bust your plateau? *It may*, but it's not a guarantee. Will taking the stairs at work make you magically lose a pound every week? Probably not. Will skipping your afternoon soda make your pants feel loose? Nah, I doubt it. Yet, *you will feel better.*

The "magic" happens when you're doing a combination of *all* of these small things. The small things add to the bigger picture, in which you already have control over. That's right; you're already doing the bigger things. Now focus on the smaller things *and the big things will happen*—as long as you're willing to rise and hustle in the smaller details.

How Many Tabs Do You Keep Open?

I remember submitting my resume numerous times before I went out on my own.

Even when I wanted to go to another department at my corporate job, I still had to submit a resume. You probably know the staples: detail oriented, great at multi-tasking, team player.

Listen carefully: "multi-tasking" isn't necessarily a talent. It's a waste of your time.

Let me ask you something: How many tabs do you normally have open in your browser? How many documents do you typically have open?

The more you have open, the *less* productive you'll be.

I challenge you to work on *one* thing at a time today. You'll easily double, even triple your productivity, plus you'll drastically reduce your stress.

When it's time to work on a project, work on your project.

And, when it's time to be with your family, that laptop better be closed.

Multi-tasking—it's over-rated.

One thing at a time with clear-cut focus; that's how you rise and hustle.

Sorry Stephen

Back in middle school, I would hang out in the courtyard in front of the school. My friends and I would have beatboxing *throwdowns*, with one person doing the rapping, and the other doing the beatboxing. My beatboxing skills have diminished [due to lack of practice,] but I'm still pretty decent.

One day, after we were done, we talked about nerds. I was asked, "Who is the nerdiest person you know?" Shamefully, I played along; although it didn't feel right. I blurted out, "Stephen; that guy is a nerd for sure." I then turned around and guess who was standing right there? Yep. Stephen.

"Hey man! Don't worry, I'm a nerd, too," I said, while trying to cover up the hateful words that would be enough to sting any 8th grader.

We continued to be friends, but you know what? I still think of that moment to this day and regret it.

That's how powerful words are.

You might not be a beatboxer in middle school, but perhaps you're at the water cooler at work and the temptation to throw someone under the bus just to "be cool" might be there.

Trust me, it's not worth the guilt. Besides, read this:

> **Do not let any unwholesome talk come out of your mouths, but only what is helpful for building others up according to their needs, that it may benefit those who listen.**
> —Ephesians 4:29

Don't join in the bashing; you're better than that. Rise and hustle with integrity.

Why is Slow Progress a Bad Thing?

Isn't it funny how we finally got connected to the internet in the 90s yet *we were* so happy? You would go to a website, then go take a shower while it loaded. Then, when it finally popped up, you were overjoyed with excitement.

Then came the 56K Modem. You could go to a website, make a cup of coffee, come back, and there it was: a website in all its glory, with faster speed.

And, next thing you know, you're enjoying lightning speed internet connections through cable and DSL.

The problem is, we want the same thing happening to our body. We *want* to simply plug into diet and exercise—and expect immediate results.

Only one pound this month, huh? You know what? I know of *thousands* of people that would *love* to lose one single pound. They are doing more than you and not making any progress, *yet*. But, they are keeping at it. They know they will one day experience a breakthrough.

Unfortunately, so many people quit due to the so-called "slow" progress. They don't understand the simple truth that slow progress is *still progress*.

One pound? I won't say *I am sorry*, instead, *Congratulations!*

Continue to rise and hustle.

Help! I Can't Stop Thinking!

If you're really busy, and especially if you're an entrepreneur, you deal with this issue daily.

You work even when you're "off."

Sure, you might be with your family on a random Saturday at the park, but what's going on in your mind? Numbers? Ideas?

No, there's nothing "wrong" with you. However, you can fix this.

No. 1 Do a "Brain Dump" at the end of each workday.

Whether you work for yourself or someone else, this works. Five minutes before you plan to leave, write down what you plan to work on the next day. And, if a big idea hits you, write that down, too.

No. 2 If an idea hits you when you're off; use the WunderList App

It happens all the time. You get a great idea that would help your business or your project, and you can't stop thinking about it because you're afraid you'll forget it. Download the WunderList App. This app syncs between your computer and phone, and you can add as many folders and lists as you want.

In fact, I have a list called "Rise and Hustle Ideas." Take five seconds to put that idea into the app, then quit thinking about it. It will be there when you get to it during work time. Right now, it's *family* time. Okay?

Start with those two things and later we'll continue. This is part of the **Rise and Hustle Lifestyle**.

The True Meaning of Success

Isn't it funny how many "selfies" you see on Facebook, Instagram, etc.? With YouTube, it's a game of "How far can you go?" to get a video to go viral.

Make no mistake about it, we live in a world of "Look at me, look at me." You see a friend or peer brag about how they are working 15-hour days and how sleep is over-rated. We see a relative having their picture taken with an A-list celebrity. Perhaps we find a contestant on a weight loss TV show losing six pounds a week, while you're struggling to drop just a single pound.

This is not how God measures success. He's not keeping a tally of how many "likes" you get on your Facebook post. He's not keeping an eye on how many hours you work every day. Instead in Joshua 1:8 we find, **"Keep this Book of the Law always on your lips; meditate on it day and night, so that you may be careful to do everything written in it. Then you will be prosperous and successful."**

That takes some pressure off, right? Nowhere in the Bible does it say that you will only be successful if you have a certain number of "likes" or work a certain number of hours, or even weigh a certain amount of pounds.

God put you on here on Earth for a reason—and that reason isn't to work yourself to death or accumulate "likes."

Your success is dictated by how faithfully you walk with God. *That's the true meaning of success. That's the true meaning of rising and hustling.*

Turn Around!

The number one reason why people give up so fast is because they tend to look at how far they still have to go, instead of how far they have gotten.
—Author Unknown

Early on in my 115-pound weight loss journey, I worked out at my old high school track. After a couple of months or so, I worked my way up to walk a mile.

I remember starting my 4th lap, feeling a bit overwhelmed. "Geez, I still have a full lap to go and I'm really tired," ran through my head. Honestly, I almost quit that day. That one lap was going to get the best of me and I wasn't sure I had it *in* me.

Suddenly, I almost felt ashamed. I asked myself, "C'mon, one single lap?" Then I stopped walking. I turned around and remembered something: *My fat butt just walked three full laps! I sure have come a long way!*

I immediately remembered when I first started; just one single lap would exhaust me.

Sometimes, we just need to stop, breathe, and realize how far we've come. This fuels us to continue the last mile.

Don't forget to appreciate how far you've come before you're overwhelmed with how far you need to go. This mentality is of *our* "Rise and Hustle" secret sauce.

Why a Kangaroo is More Successful Than You

Some interesting facts about the kangaroo:

They can jump as far as three times their height.

Even though they are heavy, they can reach up to 40 mph mid-bound.

But more importantly, they hardly ever move backwards. They always hop forward, in fact, when they do move backwards, it's extremely slow.

On the Australian coat of arms, the Emu and the Kangaroo were selected as symbols of Australia to represent the country's progress. They are always moving forward and never move backwards.

How far would you go if you *never* looked backwards at your past?

Always move forward. Live like a kangaroo; *they* know how to rise and hustle.

The Size of Your Audience Doesn't Matter

I have presented in front of over 500 people on a big stage. I talked about everything between physical transformations to how to start an online business. I even shared my productivity hacks at one event [even with ADD as my companion]. I also emceed my first event in 2014, and I had a blast doing this kind of thing. This is ironic considering I'm actually an introvert. Yet, when our Sunday School class was in need of an assistant teacher (someone to teach once a month), I was terrified. Typically, we'll have around 25 folks in our class. You would think it would be a breeze compared to presenting on stage with a PowerPoint to over 500 people. However, it was the subject matter that got me nervous.

ME: Me Lord? Really? Talking about your amazing power and grace? I don't have a lot of Bible verses memorized. I'm no preacher man for sure. And, this is what you want?
GOD: Yep
ME: Ah man. Okay. I'll do it.

That's when I realized that the size of the audience doesn't matter; the subject matter is what does.

To this day, as I get in front of our class, I'm still a little nervous. However, I have learned so much as I put together my lesson plans. He is grown me by leaps and bounds spiritually! My walk with Him is stronger than ever.

And, I get more "fired up" when *one* person in our class tells me that something helped them with their walk with God, versus the feelings felt under the lights, when speaking to hundreds of people at a conference.

**Each of you should use whatever gift you have received
to serve others, as faithful stewards of God's grace
in its various forms. —I PETER 4:10**

Rise, hustle, and serve.

Four-Prong Success Formula Revealed

In 2003, I made a life-changing decision that still impacts me to this day. Perhaps you've made this same decision, or *you want to* make this decision. The choice to "get in shape" or "get ripped" or any other health cliché is usually made when…

1. The New Year starts,
2. Just before spring,
3. Just before summer, or
4. Right when school starts.

Being in the industry for over a decade, I've seen the trends and 99 percent of the time, one of these four reasons are used whenever I meet a new client. For me, it was a New Year's decision. My goal was to lose 50 pounds in six months. You see, I didn't know any better. Looking back, I wouldn't have based my goals on what a scale said, but that's another story. Six months later, I dropped 75 pounds. Since then, I've lost another 40. More importantly, I've kept it off [except on the days I eat pancakes; cheat day pancakes]. Let me be transparent with you on how I lost 115 pounds, and kept it off.

There were some great days. There were also some tough days. There were *a lot* of frustrations. Some days, I even asked myself, *"Is it worth it?"* Trust me, *it is.* I've been asked well over a hundred times, "How did you do it?" There are no secrets. All it takes is this four-prong formula:

1. Persistence,
2. Consistency,
3. Focus on being better and not perfect, and
4. Celebrate the small victories.

If you're starting your own journey, I salute you. The road ahead is amazing, yet challenging. In the end, every second of victory—every second of difficulty and challenges—and every second of perseverance is worth it. To your best year ever; now go rise and hustle!

New Productivity Experiment

I'm a big time dork. One Saturday, I headed to the gym with my family. It was my day off from a workout, but my wife had to make up from a missed workout earlier in the week. So, what else do I do? Listen to a productivity podcast while shooting some hoops, #DorkAlert. The good news is, I had a breakthrough that I experimented with, which helped me be more productive. Typically, I'll schedule my day the night before or first thing in the morning. This way, I'm not on Facebook when I'm supposed to be writing. And, I call my Mom on Thursdays after my client's session; like a good boy.

But, this new method is different. Maybe it will work for you, too. I'm just testing it out [and will do so for two weeks to see how much more or less I accomplish].

Instead of planning your days the night before or the day of, do this instead. On Sunday night or early Monday morning:

1. Get out five index cards.
2. On one side, write the word *Monday*. Do this for all the other index cards (Tuesday – Friday).
3. On the other side, list out the important tasks you will do on each day.

Now stick to it. *This is the hard part.*

This means you are working on Project A on Wednesday and not Project B. Sometimes, project A can be scary, which is why you've been procrastinating on working on it.

This method solves that problem; I think. *We'll see.*

The more productive you are, the more freedom you have. The more freedom you have, the easier it is to rise and hustle.

The Truth About Prayer

Back in 2010, my wife and I found the perfect house. It was a ranch with a bonus room upstairs, where I would put my office. It was a five-minute walk to the gym I managed and trained my 25+ clients. It was absolutely perfect! Naturally, my wife and I prayed to get this house. But, at that time, I was self-employed, so we were denied a loan. We were heart-broken. I felt like I was being "punished" for being self-employed.

One year later, we found another house. They would give us a loan, but they wanted proof of a steady income from self-employment for two years. So, we had to wait. Those two years went by slowly while the neighborhood homes were being built very quickly. By the time two years rolled around, all of the houses were purchased.

In November of 2013, we found yet another house. The layout and neighborhood was better than the other two. I even envisioned our two boys enjoying the horse carriage rides they give kids in the neighborhood every year at Christmas. But, I was skeptical. I felt I've been "burned" before by getting hopes up. So, I was reluctant to get excited. Besides, we didn't have the money for a down payment *until...* I had a very good product launch in the spring of 2014, which allowed us to put the down payment. Shamefully, I was even reluctant on the day we signed the contract to close the deal. That's when it hit me. God knows what He's doing, and I can't see the big picture. And you know what? Neither can you.

May the God of hope fill you with all joy and peace as you trust in him, so that you may overflow with hope by the power of the Holy Spirit. —ROMANS 15:13

That neighborhood we looked at in 2010? It went under. The clubhouse is smothered in grass taller than humans. The windows are broken and the pool is sludge. Half of the neighborhood is nothing but empty lots. Where am I now? I couldn't imagine a better neighborhood or better neighbors.

Sometimes "No" is an answer to prayer.

God has your rise and hustle *brewing*. Just keep praying.

Why You'll Never Hear Them Say, "I See a Difference!"

I know, I know; this makes me seem like *Negative Nelly*. Yet, once you see how it works, you'll see why, and the "a-ha" to keep going. So, be angry with me now, but thank me later.

There are three "benchmarks" in your journey as you transform your body.

The politically incorrect truth is, most folks quit before they even finish Benchmark No. 1. I'll reveal why after I show you the three crucial benchmarks of your transformation.

Benchmark No. 1 is The Four-Week Mark

This is how long it takes for you to see your own body changing. In other words, it takes about four weeks to see a difference in the mirror.

Benchmark No. 2 is The Eight-Week Mark

This is how long it takes for your friends and family to notice a change.

Benchmark No. 3 is The 12-Week Mark

This is typically how long it takes for the rest of the world to notice your body changing.

More politically incorrect truth—most people are so concerned about Benchmark No. 3 they quit too soon. They are expecting the world to notice *before* themselves.

Keep rising. Keep hustling.

Free Resource to Become an Expert in Anything

I used to have a betta fish in my office named "Braveheart" because he was blue with a little black on his face. I wanted to learn how to take care of it well, so for a week or so, I read some "how tos" on caring for betta fish.

I knew he was happy. He talked to me. He said, "bloop bloop, bloo-bloo, bla bla bloop" which meant "Mikey, I am happy."

I have a friend in the fitness industry that started an online business on the side by reading about Facebook ads. My wife's friend buys furniture at garage sales, spruces them up, and sells it for a profit. You can read on how to do that, too. And, you know where you can get this *free* education? It might surprise you, and perhaps you thought these don't exist anymore: The library. *Yes, they do exist.*

If you want to start your own real estate business, then read a book on how to start your own real estate business. Find yourself in a rut? Read some inspiration. Want to cook like a boss? Read books on how to cook.

There is a world of education at your fingertips and it's all free. You now have the freedom to rise and hustle.

Don't Do It Backwards!

This is one of the most reassuring verses found in the Bible:

**Seek the Kingdom of God above all else, and live righteously, and
he will give you everything you need.**
—MATTHEW 6:32

The bad news? We only focus on the second half of that verse because—well, let's face it—who doesn't want to hear they will get everything they need?

But, let's break this down...

You seek God and do things *His* way. That's Step No.1; it's also the hardest step because we have to give up control. Step No. 2; in return, He will give you everything you need. Simple enough.

How do you seek Him?

I consider Him my CEO and I'm His employee, which is why I start with quiet time every day.

Pray consistently. You don't have to be at church to pray. You can drive and pray (keep your eyes open though). In fact, [outside of work] when I have been frustrated, I pray in my home office.

Don't be surprised if He reveals abundant clarity when you seek Him.

Seek Him and you'll find yourself rising and hustling.

Go This Far First...

If you were to drive from Florida to California, it may be overwhelming. After all, you're talking almost 3,000 miles and around 40 hours of driving.

That sounds exhausting.

However, going from Florida to Georgia? Well, that's not *so* bad. You *do* have to go through Georgia to get to California anyway. But still, Georgia to California? Gosh, that's a long ways.

Yet take a look at going from Georgia to Alabama. That's not so bad, either. Very doable. That's not too overwhelming at all. And yep, you're right. You'll have to go through Alabama to get to California.

You can actually visualize these shorter steps. It's not daunting. Challenging— yes, but not daunting.

These shorter steps get you to your final destination, too.

Why can't you look at your own transformation this way?

For example, losing 20 pounds can be overwhelming. That's a big challenge. But, losing just three pounds? That's doable.

Besides, to lose 20 pounds, you have to lose three pounds first.

Something to think about, huh?

> Go as far as you can see; when you get there, you'll be able to see farther.
> —J.P. Morgan

See. Do. Rise. Hustle.

Beware of the Sponge!

Behold—the sponge.

It will absorb whatever you wipe it with. It will absorb water. It will absorb grease. It will even absorb dirt on the counter [you didn't know you had].

And, when you squeeze it? It puts out *whatever* it absorbed.

Imagine wiping a sponge over some nasty grease that got caked onto your pan. Now imagine taking it over to your friend and squeezing it over their head.

Pretty nasty.

Warning: Your mind is like a sponge.

Absorb negativity from people around you, and negativity will be spilled out from you.

Absorb doubt and fear, and people will see nothing but doubt and fear coming out from you.

And just like a sponge, your mind can only absorb so much.

Choose what you absorb wisely.

It will affect how you rise and hustle.

Facing Your Giants

He loves to wake you up in the middle of the night just to watch you worry. He will sneak up behind you and whisper in your ear, "You just aren't made for this." He thrives on doubt and fear. The more you feed him, the bigger he grows. The bigger he grows, the more he dominates your every step.

We all need to face our Goliath.

But, that's where we fall. We choose to face Goliath before we face God.

It's like going into your first boxing match against Evander Holyfield without ever training.

How do you train? *You pray.*

Pray for clarity. Pray for guidance. Pray for direction.

Then, He'll show you what to do with your Goliath...

> **Blessed be the Lord my Rock, who trains my hands for war, and my fingers for battle—my loving kindness and my fortress, my high tower and my deliverer, my shield and the One in whom I take refuge, who subdues my people under me.**
> —Psalm 144:1-2 (NKJV)

... and frankly, you'll kick Goliath's butt...

> **Behold, I give you the authority to trample on serpents and scorpions, and over all the power of the enemy, and nothing shall by any means hurt you.**
> —Luke 10:19 (NKJV)

So rise with prayer. End your day with prayer.

Take down your Goliath. *And,* this is what we identify as *some serious rising and hustling.*

Why More Reps is Just Stupid

The "challenges" on social media are getting out of control.

Hundreds of pushups. Hundreds of back-breaking sit-ups. Hundreds of squats. It's redundant and ridiculous.

Let me tell you how it works:

Your 8th rep should be just as good as your first rep. If it's not, you've done too many reps.

More is not better. More is just stupid.

You're wreaking your body with horrible form, and you're going to cause an injury.

I can't even remember the last time I've seen someone do 10 perfect pushups. Sure, they might be doing 30, 40, 50 and more, but they are sloppy.

Sloppiness won't change you.

When you do your exercises (you do exercise, *right?*), choose quality over quantity *every* time.

You'll get better results with 10 perfect bodyweight squats than you would with 100 sloppy ones.

In the world of rising and hustling, we embrace quality over quantity.

Please Do Not Disturb

Our family doesn't go out much. You can imagine the struggle of going out with two young kids. So, when we do go out, it's a treat.

Yet, what I saw on our recent outing was *so* sad. At one table, I saw a Dad with his son asking him questions, while the Dad would respond with "Mmm, hmm," while staring at his phone.

Another table had a woman with two of her daughters and all three were practically doing synchronized phone viewing. All of them, with their necks down, had their right hand extended in front of their face, holding their smart phone.

Yet another table—a couple—in their mid to late 30s, with phone in hand, ignored everything in the real world, consumed by the digital realm.

I just don't get it. Perhaps I'm old fashioned. But, whether I'm out to eat or at the dinner table at home, I'll put my phone on "Do Not Disturb."

Your family in the real world should be more important than what's going on in the digital world.

I challenge you to use the "Do Not Disturb" feature on your phone, *tonight*, at dinner.

Get to know your family a little more. That's how you #RiseandHustle.

Very Important 25-Minute Task

One of the items on my bucket list is to see the Grand Canyon. I've never been and the vision of it fascinates me. I've been known to occasionally look at the live webcam at the park. Now, when the time does come for me to visit its grandness, do you think I'll just hop in my car with my family and just go? I guess I could find a road that goes west and just, *head right*? I don't know where we would stay overnight. I could just wing it. I'll find something. Oh, what about my pets? Perhaps I could call my neighbor while I'm on the road and get her to watch them? Who knows? I'll figure that out.

Sounds silly?

Instead, I'll need to visualize when we'll go. I'll need to figure out the precise directions to arrive there, too. I'll also need to book a room at a hotel and set aside plans to have our pets taken care of. I will surely need to create a vision for this trip. And to think, this would happen when we visit the Grand Canyon.

Do you have a vision for your life? Your life is far more important than a trip to the Grand Canyon. How do you want to impact the world? What are your plans for a legacy?

> **And the Lord answered me: "Write the vision; make it plain on tablets, so he may run who reads it."**
> —Habakkuk 2:2

Here's an important 25-minute task to do in the morning, when you're focused, with no distractions. That means no phone, TV or internet. Just you, some paper and a pen—and of course, a cup of coffee. Create your life vision. Stumped? Start with these questions:

What kind of legacy do you want to leave your children and family? What are your dreams [no matter how crazy they sound]? What are your talents and how can you use them to help this world? What talents would you like to develop?

This is a good place to start your life vision. Then, be encouraged. Why? Because God said:

> **For still the vision awaits its appointed time; it hastens to the end—it will not lie. If it seems slow, wait for it; it will surely come; it will not delay.**
> —HABAKKUK 2:3 (ESV)

Now go forth, rise, and hustle.

This Is the Right Time

Stop this crazy nonsense:

"Well, I can't start this week because I'll be busy with _____."

"I'll need to wait until _____ because I have _____ next weekend."

"Once I have more time, I'll be able to start my regimen."

I really like that last one. It's as if suddenly, we're going to be given an additional hour per day. Will stores be open *25-7*?

There is no perfect time to start.

There will always be obstacles. There will always be challenges.

Do you change plans of going on a road trip because there's rain in the forecast, and you don't want to drive in the rain?

Do you stop a wedding because your cousin's cousin won't be able to make it because she's sick?

Do you skip eating lunch because the restaurant you were planning on eating at is closed?

Of course not.

Do you know the right time to get in the best shape of your life? It's now. It's not next Monday. It's not two months from now. It's today.

Embrace the obstacles standing in your way. There's ways to crush them. But, for crying out loud, stop waiting for the perfect time. There is no such thing.

Any time is the perfect time to rise and hustle.

But There's 500 People!

In high school, I was in the drum line. My drum instructor encouraged me to try out for the Atlanta Drum and Bugle Corp.

This would be the next step after graduating high school. It's pretty much the "Professional Drum Line" if you will. And, they were offering two weekends to try out.

The first weekend, there seemed to be around 500 people trying out for the drum line. They were the "cream of the crop" drummers.

I was intimidated.

When I returned, my drum instructor asked, "How did it go?" I told him, "There were like 500 people there. I don't see myself making the cut with all that talent. I won't even bother coming back next weekend for round two of the tryouts."

I'll never forget what he said next and it has stuck with me for years: "You know, that's what the other 499 people think too."

And just like that, he taught me a valuable lesson on self-doubt.

Oh, that dangerous self-doubt. It's a poison that when you drink it, can hold you back from dreaming bigger.

Instead, drink a healthy dose of encouragement from the mentors and peers in your life. It's the antidote to the self-doubt poison. Take it daily to eliminate doubt and to effectively rise and hustle.

The One Word That Will Change Your Life as a Verb

A religious man is on top of a roof during a great flood. A man comes by in a boat and says "Get in, get in!" The religious man replies, "No, I have faith in God, He will grant me a miracle." Later the water is up to his waist and another boat comes by and the guy tells him to get in, again. He responds that he has faith in God and He will give him a miracle. With the water at about chest high, another boat comes to rescue him, but he turns down the offer again because "God will grant him a miracle." With the water at his chin, a helicopter throws down a ladder and they tell him to get in. Mumbling with the water in his mouth, he again turns down the request for help. He arrives at the gates of heaven with broken faith and says to Peter, "I thought God would grant me a miracle and I have been let down." St. Peter chuckles and responds, "I don't know what you're complaining about, we sent you three boats and a helicopter!"

Classic joke, but it does prove a *grand* point: Faith is an action verb.

If you have a miserable relationship with someone and you keep telling God, "Lord, please fix this," without having the difficult conversation, there's a strong chance it won't happen. Perhaps you saw that person recently and hid. Hmm, perhaps that was God's way of putting that person in your path so you can talk? God would have given you the words to say. Remember, faith is an action verb.

Perhaps you've been asking God for a breakthrough in your business. I remember being a brand new personal trainer years ago, asking God for clients. He told me to start talking to people at the gym and show them how to use the equipment. That wasn't comfortable, but faith is an action verb. He blessed me with a full schedule within a few weeks.

Do you ever hesitate stepping into an elevator to take you up? Of course not. You have faith that the elevator will take you up to where you need to be, without crashing down. Nevertheless, you still have to *step in* for it to happen. *Faith is an action verb.*

In the same way, faith by itself, if it is not accompanied by action, is dead. —JAMES 2:17

If you trust an elevator, why can't you trust God? He can take you much higher than that elevator. You just have to take that first step. Rise and hustle, with action.

Welcome Back to School

Remember back in school when we would get those Progress Reports? They typically came at the halfway point before getting our report card.

It's interesting, when we got our progress report, immediately we would realize, "Oh man, I better get my act together."

Instantly, we found enough time to invest in studying and doing our homework to bring up our grades. Yes?

Now, imagine using this kind of power with your health.

Wow.

Seriously, imagine connecting with a friend that wants to achieve similar goals as you do by a certain date. Every few weeks, you get to grade each other on your progress. You'll miraculously find more time to invest in your health. That's how those pesky, annoying progress reports work.

Set a deadline date of 12 weeks from now.

Every two or four weeks, you get graded.

Whew. That's intimidating.

But, that's just one way you can achieve greatness. It's also one way to seriously rise and hustle.

Do You Have an Outlet?

When you plug something into an outlet, it suddenly has a surge of power.

For example, without an outlet, a lamp doesn't turn on. If it's not plugged in, it simply won't work.

We are the same way.

You work HARD whether you're a stay-at-home mom, a busy executive or an entrepreneur. You need a recharge. That's where an outlet comes in.

At least one hour per week, enjoy an outlet. For me, it's basketball in the mornings at my church, three days a week.

Here are more ideas:
> *Running*
> *Yoga*
> *Biking*
> *Sewing*
> *Reading*
> *Sports*
> *Girl's Night Out*
> *Guy's Night Out*

You get the idea.

You'll be surprised at how productive and focused you become when you recharge. You *deserve* it.

> *People rarely succeed unless they have fun in what they are doing.*
> —Dale Carnegie

Don't be afraid to "get away" so you can rise and hustle.

Miss Fox's House

I have a ridiculous fear of bugs. When I see a spider in the house, I practically jump onto a chair and beg my wife to save me. One of my biggest fears came to a reality several years ago at Miss Fox's house. For a church project, our Sunday School class decided to clean her home. My mouth dropped when we walked in Miss Fox's trailer home. *Piles of magazines covered the floor, dirty clothes smothered both beds, hamster droppings were in the bed sheets, and expired milk with old food rotting were on the refrigerator shelves.*

When we were cleaning the kitchen, my friend Matt moved the refrigerator to clean behind it. Dozens of cockroaches scattered everywhere. Matt knew my phobia and saw my ghostly white face, as sweat started to drip down my nose. Miss Fox was living in this 24/7, unable to move much. She had no family to come and help her. She didn't have any close friends. She didn't have the money to pay someone to fix this stuff. Tears rolled down her face in pure joy as she saw her floor for the first time in months. Her kids no longer had to sleep in filth. New groceries filled her refrigerator and pantry.

Just curious: Do you have a "Miss Fox" in your life? It doesn't have to be a house-cleaning situation. It can be an encouraging word, a thank-you card, or simply buying someone [going through a rough patch] a cup of coffee.

**In everything I showed you that by working hard in this manner
you must help the weak and remember the words of the Lord Jesus,
that He Himself said, 'It is more blessed to give than to receive.'**
—Acts 20:35 (NASB)

Rise and hustle to help a "Miss Fox" in your life. You'll gain some perspective.

Today's Practice

Let me ask you something: If you never played a game of football in your life and you were asked to play quarterback for an NFL team, how would you do?

Probably horrible, right?

Well, getting in shape [and staying in shape] is just like any sport. It takes practice to get better. You can't expect to get on the field and throw like Peyton Manning. It takes practice.

Going from pizza and ice cream to fish and green beans overnight doesn't happen. You have to "practice" making better decisions.

Your outcome is dictated by how well you practice.

Your first couple of weeks or even months might be ugly. But the more you practice, the better you get. Then over time, these better decisions become more natural because of your consistent practice.

And *yes*, even after you get good at it, you have to continue practicing (just like a sport). If not, your skills [and your decision making] will get rusty and you'll have to start over.

That's how it works. Every day is practice.

I hope today's practice is good; and may you rise and hustle with pride as you stride.

Are You Taking This For Granted?

If you only got five minutes with your children last night, be thankful you don't have to go months without seeing them, like so many.

If you're frustrated with the traffic to get to work, be thankful you have a job. Thousands of people would love to suffer through some traffic right now.

If you're stressed about your finances, be thankful for having just a few dollars; this makes you richer than most on Earth.

If you're annoyed that your friend won't call you back, be thankful you have another friend you can confide with. There are a lot of people who are living alone on a park bench right now, dying to talk to someone.

If you're "over" the dreary rain, be thankful for your sight that lets you know what a sunny day looks like. This means, you have something to look forward to.

One day does not justify what all you should be thankful for. Be thankful, every day.

As for me, I don't resent getting up at 4 am today. I'm thankful I have the freedom to rise and hustle.

37 Words You Should Always Remember

We yell and scream about a coffee shop's choice for their logo, yet we sit in silence as teenagers and even children are used in sex trafficking.

We bury ourselves in stats to keep up with our fantasy team, who we will more than likely *never* meet, yet we have no idea that our neighbors are hurting.

We scroll, and scroll, and scroll our social newsfeed only to be fed political rants and negativity, yet we don't have any quiet time to feed ourselves encouragement and hope from His Word.

We visit "how to" sites to learn something new so we can "keep up with the Joneses," yet we don't ask God how to use the talents and gifts we already have so we can add value to the world.

> **Do not conform to the pattern of this world, but be transformed by the renewing of your mind. Then you will be able to test and approve what God's will is—his good, pleasing and perfect will.**
> —Romans 12:2

These *37 important words* are the best way to authentically rise and hustle.

The Worst Situation Before Any Health Regimen

Back in the day when I trained 25+ one-on-one clients at a gym in Dallas, GA, the first session was the easiest.

We talked. We didn't lift anything. We didn't get on a treadmill. We just talked.

I would ask them *why* they chose to get in shape. I had to investigate to figure out their expectations and more importantly, get them to believe they could do it.

You see, the worst thing you could ever do before starting or even continuing a health regimen is *not* believe in yourself.

The root of not believing in yourself is ridiculous expectations.

You've probably seen something like this: Three-day fat flush so you can lose 10 or more pounds in three days. So, you do this three-day "flush" and don't lose a single pound. Suddenly, you don't believe you can do this, and you quit.

And, that's too bad.

Before you pick up another weight, before you hop on that treadmill, before you take a bite of that grilled fish, you must set *realistic* expectations.

Then, when you crush them and think it's too easy— well, set your expectations a little higher.

Who said anything about your expectations being permanent?

Now just go, rise, and hustle.

The Difference Between Success and Mediocrity

Mediocre \ me·di·o·cre \ mē-dē-ˈō-kər \ adjective: of moderate or low quality, value, ability, or performance. Not very good.

Success \ suc·cess \ sək-ˈses \ noun: the fact of getting or achieving wealth, respect, or fame. The correct or desired result of an attempt.

Mediocre people complain they don't have enough time to achieve their dreams.
Successful people get up earlier to work on theirs.

Mediocre people suffer in silence and are too prideful to ask for help.
Successful people aren't afraid to ask for guidance from their peers and mentors.

Mediocre people wait until the New Year to accomplish any goal.
Successful people don't use a calendar to dictate their efforts.

Mediocre people watch TV more than they read.
Successful people read more than they watch TV.

Mediocre people complain about their circumstances.
Successful people do something about it.

Mediocre people "float" about their day, winging it with no plan in place.
Successful people wake up ready to attack their day with a specific plan.

Mediocre people constantly say, "I *should* do that."
Successful people are constantly doing, *that*. In other words, successful people...

Rise and hustle... and succeed.

How to Fix "Worry Wart Syndrome"

You might be worried about tomorrow while God is pruning for something big a week from now. You don't see the big picture, but God does. Let him work. —Mike Whitfield

Our lives are smothered in worry. Finances. Health. Our children's safety. Terrorism. Fighting with our spouse.

And God, the best problem solver in the world, is at our beckoning call, just a prayer away, yet we find ourselves trying to overcome worry on our own. When we are struggling financially, we turn to food or drinking. When our child is sick, we go to the internet for answers. When we fight with our spouse, we look for a friend to vent to. It's our human nature to solve it on our own. Instead, we should:

**Come to me, all you who are weary and burdened, and
I will give you rest.**
—MATTHEW 11:28

Replace worry with prayer? Is it really that simple? It is. We're just stubborn in our human ways. The next time you're smothered in worry, I suggest you read this verse:

**Therefore I tell you, do not worry about your life, what you will eat
or drink; or about your body, what you will wear. Is not life more
than food, and the body more than clothes? Look at the birds of
the air; they do not sow or reap or store away in barns, and yet
your heavenly Father feeds them. Are you not much more valuable
than they? Can any one of you by worrying add a single hour
to your life? —MATTHEW 6:25-27**

Rise, hustle, and cast your anxieties on Him.

Ride the Momentum Train

Let's pretend you're over 300 pounds. I tell you that you need to lose 115 pounds or you're going to live a miserable life. That means you'll have to give up your pancakes. And, even though you don't know what you're doing, you'll need to go to the gym three days a week.

And, *that candy bar you have in the afternoon*—you'll have to give that up, too. Not to mention your favorite soda you get on the way to work.

It's a little overwhelming, right? By the way, this applies to those who need to lose 10-15 pounds.

Let's change that. This week, take the stairs instead of the elevator.

Next week, let's aim to change out the candy bar you have in the afternoon with an apple and some peanut butter.

Then the following week, the soda you get at the gas station on the way to work every day? Let's change that for an ice-cold unsweetened tea.

Perhaps the following week, you can exercise with your friend. That could be fun.

This sounds a little easier to stick to, huh?

Here's the kicker; the result will be the same. *I'm living proof.*

Small Steps = Great Victories

Ride the **Momentum Train**. Choo-Choo. Rise and hustle.

How to Know When You've Lived Your Purpose

Have you ever asked yourself, "Am I living my purpose?" I used to drive myself crazy asking this when I worked at a corporate job I absolutely hated. I would start getting the "Monday Blues" as early as Saturday morning. Surely, this wasn't it. There had to be something better.

Suddenly, I found myself working with my Dad. After this work experience, I got the entrepreneurial spirit. I started my own fitness business as an independent personal trainer, worked in people's homes, and then found my way into a small-family gym. Now I have an online business, helping thousands of men and women all over the world, and this gives me the freedom to start the Rise and Hustle Project.

You see, I *had* to go through *that* corporate job to know how to help busy folks achieve better health; even if they work crazy hours at a job they hate. My corporate job gave me "hands on" experience. Working with my Dad, taught me valuable skills as an independent business owner. And, while training people in their homes, I learned to teach *individuals* how to achieve better health in the comfort of their own home, without equipment.

If you're *going through the motions* and wondering, *is this really it*—it's not. You're on a path to something bigger and better. You just can't give up and be satisfied. You're being "pruned" for the bigger picture and Richard Bach explains it best, "Here is a test to find out whether your mission on Earth is finished: If you are alive, it isn't."

Keep rising. Keep hustling. Your purpose will find *you*.

The No. 1 Book That Covers Everything

I love the "Super Store" concept. In the past, you would have to go to one store for the milk and eggs, then another store for home improvement supplies, then finally the Post Office for some stamps. Now, you can get all of this in one place; saving you headaches and frustration, and most importantly time. Don't you wish the same thing applied to books?

There are books for finances.
There are books for relationships.
There are books for parenting.
There are books for success and motivation.

It can be overwhelming. After all, you probably want to improve in all of these areas. Who doesn't? *However, let me tell you about one single book that covers it all.*

Dozens of authors wrote it over 1,500 years ago. Over five billion copies have been sold and distributed. The pages make a cool *crunchy* sound when you turn them; well, at least I think so.

It's called the Bible. Need help on finances? God gives you direction with over 2,000 verses. Have a desire to improve your relationships or even restore them? He has you covered. Need help parenting? Get inspiration and wisdom from His Word. Psalms is a good place to start. Motivational quotes are great, but how can you beat God's promise found in Jeremiah 29:11? It's my favorite motivational quote of all time:

"For I know the plans I have for you," declares the Lord, "plans to prosper you and not to harm you, plans to give you hope and a future." —JEREMIAH 29:11

By the way, there's a difference between some random quote from a book and a promise. I'll take His promise any day. Every morning, I'll rise and hustle to read the *best* book ever—you should, too.

Don't Rely on This One Tool

I once had a client that dropped two dress sizes. Yet on the scale, she had only lost a whopping five pounds. And yes, she was upset about the five pounds.

Her clothes were looser. She had more energy. Her cravings had subsided. Yet that scale was the only tool she based her success on.

It makes sense. According to the media and even our friends, that's what we're told to measure success by. In fact, one of the first things people ask when you have lost weight is, "How many pounds have you lost?"

Ever notice no one asks, *how more energetic do you feel, how much looser do your clothes feel or how much more productive and focused are you now that you have instilled these healthy habits?* These are the questions you need to ask yourself.

Indeed, the scale is one tool. But, you're measuring your progress using just *one tool?* Stop the madness. This would be like going in for our yearly review and basing our score according to how many emails we have sent.

Success is more than just a number on some random machine.

Remember this as you continue to rise and hustle.

Haters

There's always that one creep in his 40s you can catch on a random Tuesday afternoon ride.

You're both stopped at a red light and you look over, and there he is, with his window down, jamming out to Taylor Swift's "Shake it Off." He lip-synchs every single word perfectly:

"Cause the players gonna play, play, play, play, play
And the haters gonna hate, hate, hate, hate, hate
Baby, I'm just gonna shake, shake, shake, shake, shake
I shake it off, I shake it off…"

It's so creepy. I should probably stop. I just can't help myself. I face haters all the time. I bet you do, too.

The more good you do and the more effort you pour into adding value to the world, the more haters *gonna hate, hate, hate.*

You're losing weight; the haters tell you that you don't know how to have fun because you skip happy hour.

You start your own business; the haters criticize your ideas. *"That won't work. You're not thinking this through."*

You propose an idea at work and the haters roll their eyes. Here's the truth about haters:

> *Haters see you step out of your comfort zone and they are jealous because they are not willing to step out of theirs. —Mike Whitfield*

"Preach it Mikey," says my imaginary encourager. So what do you do? You shake it off. You shake, shake, shake it off. Then continue your…

Rise, rise, rise and hustle, hustle, hustle.

Odd Little Lesson from Grass?

It's more annoying than a long traffic light, and you wonder how in the world it got there.

It's supposedly impossible, but there it is—staring at you in the face—practically wearing a smile on its green sleeve. Grass; it miraculously grows through your driveway.

It's frustrating. You plant a garden. Nurture it with mountains of the most expensive soil you can find at Home Depot, keep it watered daily—and voila, the cucumbers and tomatoes are dead.

Yet, you drown that grass in your driveway with grass killer. You then pull it out and if the neighbors aren't looking, yell some questionable words at its existence.

Days later, the grass is back with that grin on its green sleeve, *again*.

God really wants that grass to thrive.

Hey, what about you? Do you think He wants you to thrive?

Perhaps thick helplessness is enveloping you like concrete? Do you feel stuck and trapped, not able to see the brightness of a new day?

No worries, you'll be wearing a smile on your sleeve soon. I'll let Matthew explain:

> **If that is how God clothes the grass of the field, which is here today and tomorrow is thrown into the fire, will he not much more clothe you—you of little faith?** —MATTHEW 6:20

Soon, you'll be cracking through the concrete of life, showing the world you know how to rise and hustle.

Why You Should Never Do It "Their" Way

You can imagine the "cut throat" style in the fitness world. You've probably seen the madness.

"My way is the only way."
"Any other exercise program won't work."
"Their diet stinks. That's why mine is better!"

If you're trying something new just because some expert said "it's their way or the highway," you're doing it for the wrong reasons. I'd love to tell you that my exercise programs I design are the only way to live a healthier, leaner life. But you know what? It's not, and I'm okay with that. Someone that likes to spend 60 minutes in a gym five or six days a week will not like my programs that are typically three days a week for around 30 minutes. And, if someone doesn't like full-body workouts, they will end up despising mine. And, I'm okay with that, too.

Frankly, if someone tells you the only way to get healthy is *their* way, they have an ego problem.

I give you permission to do what works *for you*. You like a combination of low carbs, Yoga, and strength training? Go for it. You dig intermittent fasting? Keep going with it. At the end of the day, it comes down to this.

1. Is it getting you results?
2. Is it something you can stick to?

Once you answer "yes" to those two questions, you got it made.

Oh, and don't forget: Enjoy the journey. Enjoy the rise. Enjoy the hustle.

The Ugly Truth About Entrepreneurship

It's interesting when I tell people what I do for a living. When they hear I have an online business, their imaginations run wild with pics of me inside a coffee shop working on my laptop, or sleeping until 10 am, or working just two hours a day, wearing a Hawaiian shirt and sandals [with socks]. But, here's the truth about entrepreneurship:

No. 1 You Don't Work on a Laptop in a Coffee Shop All Day...

...unless you want to destroy your productivity. Sure, you'll go to one every once in a while to spark your creativity, but you certainly won't spend all day there if you actually want to get something done. You need silence so you can grind it out.

No. 2 You Either Get Up Early or You Stay Up Late

My alarm went off at 4 am, just like it does every day. I had to work on my business either before or after work just like you. Yep, it's a grind. I still get up at four because I have gotten used to it; and I'm glad I did. Hint: Your brain is dead at the end of the day. Get up early to work on your business.

No. 3 You'll Be Working Even When You're Not Working

Let me explain: My brain goes 100 mph. I could be in line at a gas station, getting a coffee on a random Sunday morning before church, and an idea will hit me. Your brain will do the same. It will drive you crazy; yet it's awesome. Some days, you'll plan to "clock out" at a certain time, yet you find yourself in a groove and you don't want to mess up your flow. So, you end up working two hours later than planned.

Entrepreneurship takes tenacity. It takes guts. It takes persistence. Doubt and fear prey on it, but you battle it with courage and hustle. The payoff is huge. You control your own destiny. You live a life of purpose. And, it lets you rise and hustle how *you* choose to rise and hustle.

I Thought She Was Raptured!

In Gary Chapman's book, *The 5 Love Languages*, he explains how there are five different love languages: Words of affirmation, acts of service, receiving gifts, quality time, and physical touch.

For example, your wife may feel more loved when you spend an afternoon with her (quality time). Or perhaps your husband feels *really* loved when you tell him he is a great leader (words of affirmation). Perhaps you may end up with a spouse like mine that requires more of all five. It's difficult, but it can be done.

I once told my wife she was an amazing, Godly woman while making her dinner. This was after giving her a Starbucks gift card, for no reason, and telling her I would be willing to watch *Pride and Prejudice*. Then I gave her a hug. She melted—literally. There was nothing, but her clothes on the floor in an instant. *I thought it was the rapture and freaked out.* Then, I realized she would be back and I just overwhelmed her. All kidding aside: What if we applied these love languages with God? How awesome would our spiritual walk be? How fulfilled would we be?

1. I'm betting God would love it if we prayed to Him just to praise Him; not just praying when we're in trouble.
2. God would love it if you served Him by serving others.
3. He smiles when we give gifts to those in need. It doesn't have to be money, either. It can be time [which is more valuable].
4. He loves it when we have our daily quiet time with him. By the way, He's been meaning to show you something big for your life [you just haven't given Him the chance].
5. I can practically hear God saying, "Yes!" when I stop my two young boys in the middle of them chasing me, just to hug them and say, *I love you.* The best reason to do this with your family is *no reason.*

Jesus replied: "Love the Lord your God with all your heart and with all your soul and with all your mind."

—MATTHEW 22:37

Love God, love others, and that's how you rise and hustle.

Odd Three-Step Motivation Trick

Use this odd motivation trick and you'll have no choice but to drastically succeed in your health.

Step No. 1 Ask yourself: What size do I dream to be in 12 weeks from now?

Step No. 2 Write that size down, then show it to no less than five friends and/or family members.

Step No. 3 Buy no less than four outfits/dresses/jeans, etc. within 24 hours of completing steps one and two. The size you buy must match what is written in Step No. 2.

By the way, 12 weeks from now, you won't be able to return that stuff.

> *Formulate and stamp indelibly on your mind a mental picture of*
> *yourself as succeeding. Hold this picture tenaciously and never permit it*
> *to fade. Your mind will seek to develop this picture!*
> *—Dr. Norman Vincent Peale*

Let's go to work. Rise and hustle.

Would You Like 90 Minutes More a Day?

If you follow these four simple rules, you'll suddenly find yourself, with at least, an additional 90 minutes per day.

Rule No. 1 At the End of Each Day, Write Your To Do List for Tomorrow.

Taking five or 10 minutes to write down your most important tasks for the next day, *will keep you focused*. Put an asterisk (*) next to your top priority. This should be the first thing you work on the next day. Which brings me to my next point...

Rule No. 2 Work On Your Most Important Task First, No Matter What.

Don't you dare open your inbox or Facebook. Work on that No. 1 priority first, for at least 60 minutes. I learned this strategy from one of my mentors, Craig Ballantyne. Working on your No. 1 priority in the morning for 60 minutes is more productive than working on it for three hours in the middle of the day.

Rule No. 3 Quit Acting Like a Social Media Junkie.

There's no reason you need to be on social media for three hours a day. Look, I get it. Social media is fun. I'm not saying eliminate it. But, schedule your "fun" time. If you're on it multiple times a day, start cutting back. Fifteen minutes in the morning, 15 minutes in the late afternoon... boom. Done. *Lookie here*: I lied. If you're on social media three hours a day and cut back to just 30 minutes, you now have an additional 2.5 hours a day. *You're welcome.*

Rule No. 4 Check Your Email Twice a Day.

I check my inbox in the morning, then again in the late afternoon. Anything more is obsessive and a waste of time. If someone has something really urgent, they have your cell phone number and can call or text you. And, you know what? I can bet it's really not that urgent. Fifteen minutes here, 15 minutes there. What a waste. Quit dabbling. Dominate your inbox in your two windows. Close your other tabs. Get it done. Move on.

That's how you *crush it* every day. And, that's how you rise and hustle.

Haunted Faith

The last haunted house I went to was 18 years ago. I had to stand in line for around 45 minutes. Yep, I chose to wait so that I could walk through a house full of strangers, wearing masks, popping up, and scaring me. You don't quite know what to expect. You have adrenaline going and curiosity is killing you. You know you'll be scared out of your mind, yet understand you'll come out of the house, *unharmed*. You're doing it to take your mind on a thrill ride. You turn one corner and there's a man in a mask holding a chainsaw. You turn another corner and there's a ghost looking right at you. Now imagine if you paid $15 to $20 just to walk through a house and nothing happened.

All the lights are on. It's quiet and peaceful. Perhaps there's a TV going in the background showing a sitcom like *Three's Company* (the episode where something was misunderstood). I bet you would leave this so-called "Haunted House" very disappointed. There was no thrill. There was no, "Ah, I made it!" at the end. Just curious—why can't we treat our faith in God the same way?

We don't know what to expect at the corners in a stranger's house and we're okay with that, but when it comes to the *corners of life*, we want to know exactly what to expect. We go confidently into a haunted house knowing we'll come out just fine. Why can't we have the same confidence in our own home knowing that God is in control and yes, that *we will* indeed be fine? I believe we all need the same faith we have in haunted houses.

Now faith is confidence in what we hope for and assurance about what we do not see.

—Hebrews 11:1

By the way, the faith found in these two verses are free of charge. Faithfully rise and hustle. You'll be *just fine*.

Why You Should Enjoy Sugar
Without Feeling Guilty

Every day, I enjoy at least one cup of coffee at home. Most of the time, it's two.

I use regular creamer. It's not organic and it has a few ingredients I can't even pronounce that are supposedly "the devil" according to the media.

One of my favorite things to eat after a great workout is a peanut butter and jelly sandwich on Ezekiel Bread. I use a little less than a tablespoon of jelly. And yes, it has a few "evil" sugars.

And, you know what? I also like *not feeling guilty* when I'm not perfect. You should try it. It's awesome.

You see, when you focus on progress and not perfection, your journey to better health becomes so much more enjoyable.

Choosing coffee with a little creamer surely beats a Mr. Pibb and an iced honeybun [aka, my old breakfast] every day.

That's victory. And, it's a victory I've enjoyed for years now. It's not perfect. But, I also don't expect myself to be perfect.

That's how I rise and hustle, *without the guilt*. Try it.

Do This Every 90 Days

I went to my first "mastermind" in 2011. They're pretty intimidating. You sit at a large table with other folks that desire to push their online business to the next level. Back then, I was a rookie without a single product sold online, sitting next to those that have built full-time incomes using the power of the internet. I was "scurried" as the cool kids say. I was so nervous, my voice was shaky when I explained where I wanted my business to go.

If you were to ask me if I would do it all over again, I'd say: *Yup*, without hesitation. *Why? How powerful is a mastermind?* Within six months, I quit my personal training job [with the exception of my superstar client of over eight years now], and quit managing the gym. A few weeks after that, my wife quit her job as a teacher and became a Stay-at-home Mom, due to my online business.

Do I have your attention? Good. This what you do: Every 90 days, spend a full day with two or 10 other people that want to achieve similar goals as you. Answer these four questions:

1. Where are you now?
2. Where do you want to go?
3. How will you get there?
4. What do you think is holding you back? In other words, what are your *bottlenecks*?

Each person lays it on the table, and you give them ideas. They do the same for you. Ninety days later, you're held accountable. You either did what you said you were going to do, or you didn't. Either way, you'll have to answer.

This "mastermind" concept works in all areas of your life. It can be business, parenting, health, spiritual, and more. In fact, I'm even part of a smaller mastermind with two of my peers. Every two weeks, over the phone, we cover it all: business, family, and our spiritual walk. We pray for each other at the end of the call. If you prefer, it doesn't have to be every 90 days—make it bi-weekly, monthly, etc. Just do it. It's way more powerful than you think.

Start a mastermind, or join one. Full speed ahead: masterminding, rising, and hustling...

If It's So Heavy; Why Are You Still Carrying It?

Imagine holding a dumbbell above your head 24 hours a day, seven days a week. This includes while you're eating, sleeping, and spending time with your family and friends. What kind of mood would you be in? Would you be tired and perhaps short-tempered? Would you be snappy and on edge? Would you be able to enjoy anything? Sounds pretty frustrating, right?

This is your world if you're hanging onto resentment.

That bitterness will be a burden above your head until you simply let it go and choose to forgive. I walked with resentment hanging over my own head when I went through a surprise divorce. I was snappy. I was short-tempered. I wasn't able to enjoy my friends and family until I finally let it go.

Let. It. Go.

> **Get rid of all bitterness, rage and anger, brawling and slander, along with every form of malice. Be kind and compassionate to one another, forgiving each other, just as in Christ God forgave you.** —Ephesians 4:31-32

By the way, once I let go of that resentment and chose forgiveness, I met my wife of over 10 years who makes me pancakes occasionally. *Forgiveness rocks.*

If your burden is so heavy, why are you still carrying it?

> *To be a Christian means to forgive the inexcusable because God has forgiven the inexcusable in you.* —C.S. Lewis

To rising and hustling, *without the burden.*

The Strange JCPenny Moment...

Years ago, while working at my corporate job, I decided to shop for a pair of jeans on my lunch break. I was in a size 46 a few months earlier; being in the 40s was a big deal because that meant I was on the verge of being in the 30s. I still remember breathing heavily in anticipation, wondering if these new size 40s would fit. I took them to the dressing room and this was the moment: One leg in. Second leg in. Now, let's see if they slide over this butt of mine. Suddenly, there they were, around my waist, *comfortably.*

I raised my fist in the air. Immediately, I called my workout partner Tom in excitement from the dressing room. "Tom! Tom! Dude! I'm in 40s! I'm calling you from the dressing room right now!" I yelled into the phone while hearing JCPenny employees chuckle in the background.

Now hear me out. This was just a highlight of my journey. I also had bumps and bruises on the way:

Frustrating plateaus...

Missing my awesome breakfast of an iced honeybun and Mr. Pibb...

Being sore from working muscles that hadn't been worked in years...

Sacrifices...

Feeling intimidated walking into the gym.

But, if losing weight and getting healthy was full of only the highlights, wouldn't everyone be successful? That's what makes your journey so special. Now it's time for one of my favorite movie quotes by Jimmy Dugan's character from *A League of Their Own:* It's supposed to be hard. If it wasn't hard, everyone would do it. The hard... is what makes it great. [For me, this is *such a good quote,* I am using it twice in this book.]

The great is what makes us rise and hustle.

The Antidote to Decision Fatigue
(Part One)

Let me tell you about "Decision Fatigue," a term coined by social psychologist Roy F. Baumeister. You see, there's a limit of mental energy for using self-control. When you fight temptation for a long period of time, you're less able to resist other temptations like yelling at your kids or saying questionable words while sitting in traffic.

You spend anywhere between three or four hours a day resisting desire and that willpower drastically *decreases* (up to 60 percent) as the day goes on. Today, you *stop* being indecisive. It's simple. Take 20-30 minutes creating your own personal rules. I have 10, but you can create as little as three just to get something started.

My mentor and friend Craig Ballantyne taught me this "trick" and it's been a life-changer. You'll drastically reduce your stress, become *way more decisive*, and you'll become extremely productive. Here are my first five rules and why I created them; they will hopefully give you some inspiration.

No. 1   I will not drink any alcohol. [It's comical to even write this because I don't like the taste of alcohol.] Why? So I can increase my productivity without brain fog.

No. 2   No more caffeine after 1pm. Why? So I could sleep better. If it's 1:15, there's no "Should I? *I don't know.*" The cut-off is the cut-off. No exceptions. I move on.

No. 3   I will start every day with prayer and quiet time. *Nothing* else will come first. Why? So it can set the tone for my day.

No. 4   Even when I'm traveling, I will tell my family I love them at least once *every* day. Why? So my family understands they are important to me and I want to remind them of that.

No. 5 I will strength train no less than twice per week, unless I'm traveling. If I am traveling, I will at least go for a walk every day. Why? Because my energy and well-being depend on it!

My challenge to you: Create a minimum of three personal rules to live by this week. Chop. Chop. Or should I say, rise and hustle?

Are You in God's Waiting Room?

Remember when you were introduced to the internet? You would load it up, go *do something*, while it connected through your phone line. You heard the strange static and buzzing followed by the infamous, "You've got mail!"

You didn't complain that it took numerous tries and at least a few minutes before you connected. Then DSL came along. *The wait* went from minutes to seconds. Suddenly, cable came along and you were on the internet instantly.

Technology is a double-edged sword. It gives us what we want *faster*, yet when it doesn't work, we get frustrated and impatient.

And, to be politically incorrect, we do the same thing with God. We pray, and then expect an instant answer.

Can you imagine if He answered our prayers instantly with exactly what we wanted every single time? Before you answer that, let me ask another question: Have you ever witnessed a young child being given anything they want after they whine for it and think, *"What a spoiled brat!"*

What would the difference be between that child and *us* if we got what we wanted when we wanted it? Yep, we would be spoiled little brats with no character. Besides, have you been waiting for a long time for an answer? *It's not as long as you imagine it to be.*

Moses waited 40 years before knowing his purpose in life. Abraham waited for 100 years before he had Isaac. Noah waited 120 years before it rained while building the ark. God promised and God delivered. You can count on God coming through for you, too. I guarantee it because the Word says so.

For the revelation awaits an appointed time; it speaks of the end and will not prove false. Though it linger, wait for it; it will certainly come and will not delay. —HABAKKUK 2:3

Rise, hustle, and wait patiently. He *will* answer you.

The Sign-Up Dare

Every year on July 4th in Atlanta, GA, a 10K is held: The Peachtree Road Race. Locals like myself call it "The Peachtree."

In March of 2003, my friend pushed me to sign up for it. I had never ran a race in my life and I was certainly not ready at the time. If I had attempted to run six miles when he asked, I would have collapsed. I had made progress, but I wasn't even close to my final destination.

Yet, I still signed up. I registered. There was no turning back. On July 4th, I would be running.

Looking back, it was just what I needed. By signing up for something I wasn't ready for, it challenged me to continue making progress, such as making better food choices and not missing my workouts.

When the big day did came, I was ready. It helped me with my long-term goals. And, that's the point I want to make. Twenty-one-day challenges are good. Seven-day jumpstarts are great. Long term goals are for the serious and they are the *best*.

Here's my dare to you: Sign up for something happening three to four months from now. Let it be something that scares you, yet keeps you on track.

A 5 or 10K...
A sprint triathlon...
A hike...
Master your first pull-up...
Master a certain number of push-ups...

You get the idea. Sign up. Rise up. Hustle up.

The Antidote to Decision Fatigue
(Part Two)

Here are my last five rules, and my whys. Let them inspire you so you can create your own:

No. 6 I will not curse. Why? I just don't see the point. I also don't want my kids cursing. I want to set an example.

No. 7 Before I make any financial, family or business decisions, I will seek the wisdom of God. Why? God is my CEO. I'm His employee. He knows the big picture and what's best for me.

No. 8 I will not work from 8 a.m. Saturday through Sunday. Also, once I'm done with my workday, *that is it*. I will not go upstairs to my office to "sneak in" more work. This includes checking my email. Why? Being an entrepreneur, I am addicted to work. Even when I was with my family, I found myself not "present" and working mentally. I had to fix that. If it's a Friday night and my wife has her "Girl's Night Out" and the boys are down, I will not ask myself, "Should I get a little work done?" I'll enjoy a book because if I work, I'll be up too late and that will affect my next day.

No. 9 I will write a to-do list before I start my day. Why? I want to focus only on what matters. If I "wing it," my day will be unproductive. This should be done whether you own your own business or not. I'm pretty sure any company would be okay with their employees being more focused and productive.

No. 10 I will end my workday by reading the following scriptures: Jeremiah 29:11; Jeremiah 33:3; Romans 12:2; Hebrews 12:11; and Psalms 32:8. Why? I call this my **Daily Attitude Adjustment**. Look those up. I promise they are worth your time.

Create your own rules; you won't regret it. After all, creating your own rules lets you rise and hustle.

By the way, you can download your *Attitude Adjustment Cheat Sheet Bible Verses* FREE here: **http://riseandhustle.com/resources/**.

The Connection Between God and a... Bike?

Imagine your child being 10 years old and wanting his first bike, but you recently got laid off.

You work odd jobs on the side, paying you very little, just to make ends meet. You're barely able to pay the bills, but you keep thinking about getting that brand new bike for your child.

You work longer and longer hours. You wait tables at night. You stock grocery shelves during the day. You work the graveyard shift on the weekends. You're exhausted, but too in love with your child to notice the fatigue.

And every day, your child comes to you asking, "Please, please, *please*. I realize I don't *need* a bike, but I know I would love to have one. My friend down the street wants me to ride with him after school. Can I get one, please?" You painfully say: *Not yet.*

Days go by...
Weeks...
Months...

Then finally, you're able to answer your child "yes" when the timing was just right. He comes home from school one day with the bike sitting in the living room.

"Thank you, thank you, thank you! Oh wow! I can't believe you got me this bike! You are the *best* Dad ever!" he says, with tears in his eyes (and yours).

It's a prideful occasion. You look at your son with pure joy, admiring this moment in time.

The next day, he comes home from school. He doesn't even give you a chance to say "hi" before he is out the door to ride bikes with his friends. He doesn't even have time to ask you what he wants next. Just like that—the moment is over.

You know what? We sometimes do the same thing to our Father in Heaven.

We spend time on our knees asking and begging for *what we think* we need, pleading for a yes. And when we get that yes, we thank Him right then and there. Then we move on.

We spend so much time asking Him, yet very little time thanking Him.

> **Praise the Lord. Give thanks to the Lord, for he is good;**
> **his love endures forever.** —PSALM 106:1

If His love endures forever, I think I'll be thankful forever. You?

Rise, hustle, and take time to be thankful.

Do Not Avoid That Stairwell

In my corporate-world days, I had a great workout partner named Greg. I believe it was Wednesdays that we went over to Building C of our corporate office, after work. Building C had 22 flights of stairs. You can probably guess what our workout was...

All the way up, all the way down...
All the way up, all the way down...

Two rounds of horrific, leg-burning, heart-pounding awesomeness.

Now you can imagine looking at 22 flights of stairs. It's rather intimidating. If I were to take you there and say, "I want you to take one big leap to the top," you would probably look at me funny, right? In fact, you might even walk away and shake your head knowing that would be impossible. However, what if I took you to that stairwell and asked you to take one flight of stairs, starting with the first step.

"Hey, I can do that," would cross your mind. That's the point.

What's *your* stairwell?

Losing 50 pounds or more?
Aiming for your first pull-up or chin-up?
A 5K or 10K?

Looking at the end result can be intimidating and overwhelming.

Just like Greg and I, simply take that first step, no matter how small.

Every step brings you closer and closer to the top of your stairwell.

Those first three pounds. Your first assisted pull-up or chin-up. Your first half mile.

Don't walk away from your stairwell. Rise and hustle to it.

When You Are Overwhelmed...

Wikipedia. Google. YouTube. Kindle. We can learn about anything we want thanks to the technology and resources at our fingertips. The bad news? This can be overwhelming.

You might be on info overload.

Yet, you may feel you'll "miss out" if you don't take action on the latest and greatest, right? *I know what this is like.* I've been there. So, here's a little "trick" on what I do.

When I stumble on a fitness article or new research that I know my fitness readers will enjoy, but I'm supposed to be working on creating a product, *I simply bookmark it.* I created a bookmarking folder called "Studies" another one is called "Fitness Article Ideas." And, if it's good content to review for my fitness business, or an "a-ha" moment from a book—I make a note. This way, I can focus on one thing at a time. Why?

Let me be blunt...

Multi-tasking is *not* productive. The more "multi-tasking oriented" you are, the less productive and the more overwhelmed you'll be.

Is that bold? You bet. And, I'm speaking from experience.

Focus on what matters most—the info will *always* be there.

In other words, if you're working in an area of your life like your relationship, but you see an article on productivity, bookmark the productivity article. Work on that relationship. Working on one thing, with diligence and discipline, gives true meaning to the **Rise and Hustle Lifestyle**.

Seven-Minute Marriage Trick

There's a seven-minute trick I've been using for the past seven months, that has made a huge, positive impact in my marriage.

Every morning, I get up at 4 am so I can have my personal quiet time and then work on important tasks in my business. On Mondays, Wednesdays, and Fridays, I need to have it *all done* by 6 am.

It's then I have a life-changing appointment with my wife. The average time this appointment takes is around seven minutes, which gives me enough time to get to my church for some pickup basketball at 6:30 am.

I sit down and ask her: *What's on your mind and what can I pray about, for you?* She then does the same for me. We share our triumphs and our struggles. We're very open. Then, we take turns praying.

Now after 10 years of marriage, you would think you would know just about everything about your spouse. Yet, here I am learning new things about her every day and honestly, it's improved my walk with God, *and my marriage.* It's like loving pancakes for years with regular syrup and discovering *real* maple syrup. You don't know what you're missing.

So here comes the infamous cliché: C'mon now, you knew it was coming: Couples that pray together stay together.

It takes as little as seven minutes. For crying out loud, you can get these minutes, by not hitting the snooze button. Try it. You'll find your life changing.

Therefore encourage one another and build each other up, just as in fact you are doing.
—1 Thessalonians 5:11

Rise, hustle, and pray for a stronger marriage.

That's a Horrible Idea

You shouldn't pile on plate after plate, just because it's some random holiday. You shouldn't go back for seconds, thirds, or fourths because you can get back on track, *tomorrow*. You shouldn't eat 15 cookies at the office party just because it's not the New Year, quite yet.

Your health runs just like a credit card. You pile on the debt of sugar and guilt and you'll have to pay for it with interest.

The next thing you know you're paying interest only for the first three months of your new health routine, instead of improving the debt you already had.

Your bill shows up in the mirror and in how you feel. Then the transactions come to mind:

Too many cookies here...
Too many drinks there...
Too many plates at that place...
Too much mindless eating at this place...

Does that mean you can't put *anything* on your health credit card? Of course not. Enjoy your time with your family. Have a couple of Grandma's cookies. Enjoy a slice of cake at the office party. You're an adult. Be responsible. Spend wisely.

That's how you rise and hustle, without the incredible debt.

Three Simple Habits That Release Your Full Potential

It was Wednesday, the day before Thanksgiving, exactly 11:33 a.m. the year 2003. I was staring at the clock with anxiety and anticipation. It felt like time was standing still. I could hardly wait to "clock out" from my old corporate job, where I was a slave behind a desk, *unappreciated*. I was waiting until noon. Then, I could clock out and take off the next few days from work to celebrate the holiday.

I was so miserable, I was already dreading going to work on Monday, as I left the building. Thank God I got out of my comfort zone and discovered my true passion and experienced the freedom and the art of entrepreneurship. I struggled when I started. Then, I stumbled on several habits from my mentors and coaches.

Here are the three habits I found to be the "norm" of the most successful people I know:

Habit No. 1 Get Up Early. For over two years now, I've been getting up at 4 am. That sounds crazy, but I get more done between four and six than most people get done in a day. Why? The world is quiet. It's just me and my goals. Nothing is in the way. You don't have to get up at four, but try getting up 30 minutes earlier to work on your dreams.

Habit No. 2 Check Your Email Twice a Day, at Most. *Refuse* to let your inbox dictate your to-do list. Your to-do list should be dictated by your dreams. The masses work on their emails before their dreams. That's the way we are wired. You must reprogram yourself to do the opposite.

Habit No. 3 Exercise Regularly. Those that are not physically active are typically the ones that have a mindset of being trapped of working for "someone else" the rest of their lives. When you're active, you have more energy, drive, and focus. Channel that into your dreams. Swim. Play basketball. Lift weights. Do *something*.

Focus on these three habits, and you'll make amazing progress this year. Trust me, you'll have enough progress where people will look at you and think, "They rise and hustle."

How to Build Spiritual Muscle

"Look, I love eating broccoli. That's right. This magic pill makes me crave broccoli. I've lost 194 pounds in just four weeks!"

"Wow, my abs are so defined and sharp, I was scratching my stomach and I cut my finger! It's all because of this new secret, groundbreaking, underground, something-something exercise workout and you can cut your finger, too!"

Outrageous fitness claims are everywhere, aren't they? Yet no one is talking about a muscle way more powerful than six-pack abs.

What do you do to stay encouraged, faithful, and hopeful? What's the point of having a six-pack if you have no hope? What's the point of going on a run, to exercise your heart, if you're still clinging onto buried resentment you can't sweat out? You're willing to release your endorphins, which is great, *but how are you releasing worry?* Just like any muscle group, you need to exercise your faith.

"But Mikey, getting a trainer is expensive!" No worries, I'm going to connect you to a special trainer and friend of mine. He's got a special going on right now where you get all the training you want for free. He gave me this workout and He said I could share it. In fact, you probably already have His training manual. Look for the book on your shelf called the *Bible*. If it's not handy, you can get all kinds of apps on your phone for *free* that show it in digital form.

Warm-up. Sit in silence and be still for one minute. Psalm 46:10 says, **"Be still and know that I am God."** Then, Do This Following Circuit:

Exercise No. 1: Praise Him for the blessings you have; including the little things we might be taking for granted like eating dinner with your family, seeing a friend, an answered prayer, and more. **Every good and perfect gift is from above, coming down from the Father of the heavenly lights, who does not change like shifting shadows [James 1:17].**

Exercise No. 2: Open up His word and read it. Not sure where to start? Go to Proverbs. If today is the 5th, read Chapter 5. If it's the 20th, read Chapter 20. You get the idea. You will be encouraged! **Commit to the LORD whatever you do, and he will establish your plans [Proverbs 16:3].**

Exercise No. 3: Pray. Don't hold anything back. Reveal your dreams to Him. Cast your worries at His feet. Why? He knows what to do with it. **For my thoughts are not your thoughts, neither are your ways my ways," declares the Lord [Isaiah 55:8].**

Do this workout every day and you'll experience more peace, clarity, and hope. Rise, hustle, and build your spiritual muscle.

A Big Mistake in Denver

A couple of years ago, I had went on business trip to Denver. After a long day of brainstorming, I went to my hotel room and ate. I was proud of myself, ordering grilled chicken breast, green beans, and some steamed rice. After that I was still hungry. I took a quick walk to a convenience store just a block away. I had the willpower to skip the doughnuts that looked delicious, but a small bag of one of my all-time favorites was staring back at me: banana chips.

"If I eat just 1/5th of the bag, it's only 150 calories," I thought. So, I grabbed it and a bottled water. On my walk back, I immediately opened the bag and ate a couple. The sugary, buttery-sweetness never tasted *so good*. I made my way up to my room, put the hotel key on the nightstand, and continued mindlessly taking bite after bite.

"Now remember, just eat 1/5th of the bag and then throw the rest away," I thought. One bite after another, the bag dwindled down to nothing. Within minutes, I ate the entire bag. That was 750 calories consumed in less than a few minutes.

Why am I telling you this? To tell you the truth. While losing 115 pounds, I struggled. And you know what? I *still* do. You want to know the *true* "secret" to a real, lasting transformation? You're going to fall flat on your face. You won't be able to go "beast mode" with every workout. You may get off your plan or miss a workout here and there. It's not a "This is so easy and fun" road like the cheesy commercials tell you. It's one battle after another. You'll lose some battles. You'll win some. Just remember, many wars have been won while losing battles.

Remind thyself, in the darkest moments, that every failure is only a step toward success, every detection of what is false directs you toward what is true, every trial exhausts some tempting form of error, and every adversity will only hide, for a time, your path to peace and fulfillment.
—Og Mandino

One bad night won't stop you just like it didn't stop me. A real transformation means you forget the lost battles and continue to rise and hustle.

The Art of The Brain Dump

If you haven't tried this, you need to. It's extremely powerful.

It's called: **The Brain Dump.**

For years, I "carried" my work into my family time. Sure, we could be at the park, but my mind was on my next *big idea* or how I should prioritize my to-do list for the next day.

I was there, but I wasn't present. There *is* a difference.

Accepting the fact that I had this problem, I asked one of my mentors, Craig Ballantyne of Early to Rise, what I could do. He suggested I do a brain dump. This is where I take a few minutes at the end of the day to write down my ideas on a piece of paper. For a while, I struggled with this, but then I got the hang of it. And you will, too.

This is exactly what you do and it's worked for me, like a charm:

1. Get a sheet of paper.
2. Write out any ideas that hit you today; no matter how "crazy" they sound.
3. Write out the Top Three priorities you need to focus on the next day.

That's it. And, don't check your inbox one last time. *Why?*

You'll see what you think is a "fire," but in reality it isn't. You then get all "worked up" and you'll have to start a brain dump, yet again. Believe me, it can wait until tomorrow.

Brain dump away, so you can rise and hustle with your family.

Snap!

The year was 1992 and 65,000 spectators jam-packed a stadium and millions of others were watching it on TV. The anticipation for years had been building up to this moment.

Athlete Derek Redmond was determined to get a medal in the 400-meter race at the 1992 Olympics. His father Jim was not only his Dad, but also his best friend, who was among the crowd cheering him on.

Just 175 meters away from the finish line—SNAP! Derek's right hamstring popped. He limped on one leg, tried to finish, but fell on the track. The medics ran toward him while his father did the same. He had no credentials to be on the track, yet that didn't stop him. He was determined to get to his hurt son so he could help him up.

The medical team offered a stretcher. Derek refused. "No way I'm getting on that stretcher. I'm going to finish my race," he said.

He continued to hobble himself down the track with every step more and more painful. His father Jim reached him about 120 meters away from the finish line. "I'm here son," said Jim as he hugged him. "We'll finish together," he added as tears streamed down Derek's face; he put his arms around his Dad's shoulders. Together, father and son embraced and made their way to the finish line.

"I'm the proudest father alive," he told the press afterwards, tears in his eyes.

This story made me think of what you're running in right now. You're making great progress and suddenly, something snaps. You find yourself crippled with doubt and fear because it's not going the way you thought it would. Perhaps you're hobbling your way through life right now; trying to make something happen.

God is on His way down from the stands of Heaven. He's going to wrap His arms around you. He'll tell you: *I'm here. We'll finish together.* It might be painful. It might not be as fast as you hoped. But, you will finish. You just need to accept His embrace.

Do not be afraid, for I have ransomed you. I have called you by name; you are mine. When you go through deep waters, I will be with you. When you go through rivers of difficulty, you will not drown. When you walk through the fire of oppression, you will not be burned up; the flames will not consume you.
—Isaiah 43:1-2 (NLT)

Rise and hustle, even if you have to hobble toward your finish line.

Don't Sue Yourself

I had a friend come to me for fitness advice on losing weight about two weeks before Halloween. When I gave him a simple nutrition *template*, he told me: "This is great. I'm really serious this time, and I am not going to cheat until Thanksgiving." Keep in mind he has four kids and a full-time job. Needless to say, the "diet" didn't work out.

And, it wasn't because he wasn't motivated, nor was it because he has a slow metabolism or his genetics. It was because of the same reason thousands of other people "fail" with any kind of fitness regimen: He set unrealistic expectations (I call this "SUE").

I see this all the time with New Year Resolutions. You might commit five or seven days a week to the gym. You might have a diet of 80 percent processed foods, but you're expecting to reverse your methods in one week.

After two or three weeks, you feel guilty because you're not doing what you said you were going to do—so you give up. And, that's a shame. Don't "sue" yourself.

Here's how to fix this.

Set up small victories, also known as "realistic expectations." For example, if you haven't seen the gym in months, commit to going two times a week for 30 minutes for the first two weeks. You can always add to it. And for crying out loud, you don't have to *re-haul* your diet, either. What are one or two things you can improve in the first week of your new regimen? Do those one or two things and that's it. This gives you momentum. Momentum gives you consistency. Consistency gives you the right to brag that you rise and hustle [even a little at a time].

Four Ways to Get More Done, *Today*

You're overwhelmed. *Bills. Exercise. Work. Kids. Spouse.* You name it. "If I didn't have a thousand things to do today, I wouldn't be so busy," says everyone, every day. Do you mind if I hurt your feelings? This is *your* fault. Ouch. Well, at least you can fix it with these four Productivity Hacks:

No. 1 Multi-Task Smarter

If you have 10 projects on your plate, get rid of nine of them today (or at the very least, put them on the back-burner). Listening to a podcast while doing laundry is smart multi-tasking. Working on a project and answering emails at the same time is not. If you're an entrepreneur, simply choose the project that will move your business the fastest. Living in the corporate world? Have the difficult conversation with your boss and work together on which projects will be put on hold.

No. 2 I Dare You to Be on Social Media for 20 Minutes, Max

I just freed up at least 90 minutes for you. Don't have the discipline? Check out some apps that are currently available: Search "self-control" and choose the one that best suits your personality.

No. 3 Walk Away Every 90 Minutes

I work from home. Every 90 minutes, I either: A. Go downstairs and get water or B. Play hide-and-go-seek for five minutes with my black lab. I throw her toy rope, she fetches it, and I hide. Yes, it is awesome and hilarious. I come back a productive beast. It's like hitting the reset button to your mind. Try it.

No. 4 Get Up Earlier

Yes it's hard. The first step is admitting it. Now get up earlier; even if it's just 15 minutes.

Such simple, actionable trickery, yet most won't do it because they think *meh*. I hope you're not a "Meh-er." Instead, rise and hustle.

I Was Caught Staring

A few nights ago, my wife and I attended a short nutrition seminar.

The information was fantastic, but one particular PowerPoint slide got my attention. The presenter discovered his son consumed what's called a "Donut Burger."

It was a big, juicy burger with donuts as the "buns"... in all its glory staring at me from the huge screen. The "ewwwws!" and chuckles flooded the entire room of 60 people. However, for me, it was a little different. I was silent with a voice that could be heard only in my head:

"Oh…that looks *so good*. Whatever you do, *don't* moan."

Then I moaned (just a little bit). It slipped. My wife elbowed me.

The voice continued:"Self-control you moron! *Mmmm... burrrrrrger and dooooonut*. Shush. You need an apple when you get home big guy."

You see, years ago, I lost 115 pounds. I've been able to keep it off, too. But it hasn't been easy. The temptations are still there.

Yet thankfully, I'm a brand *new* person who can overcome those temptations. It says so in His Word:

> **This means that anyone who belongs to Christ has become a new person. The old life is gone; behold, the new has come.**
> —2 Corinthians 5:17 (ESV)

It doesn't say in the Bible that you and I won't ever be tempted again. But, it does say we *do* have the strength to say no:

> **I can do all things through Christ, who strengthens me.**
> —Philippians 4:13 (NKJV)

The "new me" enjoys a couple of planned rewards a week. If I'm tempted outside of those planned rewards, I lean on these two verses (and it helps that I'm having to set an example for my kids, too).

Rise and hustle my friend. You *can* do all things!

Why Willpower Fails

In the health industry, we are taught to say things like, "It's not your fault." It's rare you'll ever see an expert say the words: This is *your* fault!

Ruffle. Ruffle. Ruffle. Pretend these are your feathers.

I say: When you keep setting yourself up for failure, it *is* your fault. Quit buying cookies at the store and claiming, "They are only for my cheat meals," then proceed to eating them every single day. Stop hitting that burger joint you love so much, three times a week, followed by, "I'll start tomorrow."

This might come across as rude, but sometimes we need a good, old fashioned kick in the *bohonkus* (yes, I really wrote "bohonkus"... makes me giggle like a school kid, too. #YouAreNotAlone).

The thing is, you're making things harder on yourself than they need to be.

Set up your environment for success. If you don't have cookies in your house, you won't have to constantly drain your energy fighting the temptation. Then when reward time comes, you can have one of those fancy *schmancy* gourmet cookies at a deli.

And for crying out loud, if you're so tempted at the burger joint, go another way home.

Your environment is more important than any kind of willpower. Willpower is also overrated. Just because you rise and hustle, it doesn't mean you have to wear yourself out.

Three Apps You Should Use

There are three apps that have made my life *so much easier*, especially when I travel. Now, whether you travel or not, these apps can help you stay productive and a little more organized.

App No. 1 Dropbox. It's well worth the $199 a year, but there is also a free version. Dropbox allows you to sync files between your computer, phone, and other devices. In other words, you can be working upstairs on your computer on a file. Then, let's say you want to continue working on it with your laptop. You don't need a flash drive. Just use the Dropbox App and you'll pick up right where you left off.

App No. 2 Wunderlist. I've been abusing this app on my phone. Wunderlist allows you to make multiple lists and even share them with your friends/family. I share my grocery list with my wife. That way, if I need something, I can plug it into the list, and it will show up in her app on her phone. But, it doesn't stop there. I have a problem: My brain never stops. I'm constantly thinking of new ideas, even when I'm getting in my workout or going for a walk. I don't ever want to forget them, so I instantly plug my ideas into my app.

App No. 3 Evernote. Consider this a little more elaborate than Wunderlist. It syncs across all your computers, phones, etc. The big plus: his app lets you save files as well as photos. I use this when I see an article idea for my fitness business. If I find a good article when I am reading *Men's Health* or *Women's Health*, I take a photo of the article and plug it into Evernote.

Use those apps to seize the rise and hustle advantage.

What to Ask God For

When my wife and I were dating, we got into a heated discussion about having kids. It was simple. She wanted them. I was unsure—leaning on not wanting them.

We took a risk getting married as I was still on the fence at the time. Looking back, this was really risky.

You see, I was enjoying my late dinners at 8:30 p.m., watching an episode of *Friends* [the one where Ross and Rachel have issues], and I didn't have to worry about getting up to comfort a crying child. Straight up: I think baby poo-poo is extremely gross. I didn't want to *ever* have to deal with that.

I also wanted to enjoy my little bit of video game time, creating a football team called the "Jackasses" so that whenever I beat a team, I could tell the TV, "Ha! You got beat by a bunch of Jackasses!"

"You really sharing that?" says, God's voice in my head.

Well, you know what? My wife, Sabrina and I, now have two young boys: Champ and Deakan. These two little guys are my best friends.

Come to find out, Sabrina had been praying over me. She asked God to change my heart. Apparently, it worked. I can't imagine life without these two gifts. While Sabrina was asking God to change my heart. I was asking God to change my circumstances (in other words, "Let me be selfish God!").

Sometimes, you need to ask God to change your heart and not your circumstances.

Ever thought, that perhaps, you're praying for something *against* God's will and that's why your prayers haven't been answered?

That was a good lesson God taught me through my wife. I'm glad He changed my heart.

And, this is a great place for one of my favorite bible verses of all time...

And do not be conformed to this world, but be transformed by the renewing of your mind, so that you may prove what the will of God is, that which is good and acceptable and perfect.
—Romans 12:2

And besides, God also put it on somebody's heart to invent latex gloves so I can change poopy pants. #GoGod. Rise and hustle, with a changed heart!

The Calorie Myth

Years ago, before I had lost 115 pounds, my grandfather asked me out of the blue, "Mike, do you know Jenny Craig?" I then responded with, "No, I sure don't." I though perhaps he had met her. Then he said, "You should get to know her."

Hilarious Paw-Paw—so hilarious.

And you know what? I never got to know Jenny Craig, and I still lost 115 pounds. So let me tell you about this whole "Calorie Myth" hogwash.

A calorie is *not* just a calorie and it's more than "calories in and calories out."

Example:

Option A: Just 2½ small chocolates equal approximately 110 calories. Approximately 44 calories per piece + 22 calories for another half piece.

Option B: Two small, cold, and crisp Gala apples equals approximately 110 calories. Approximately 55 calories per apple.

Hmm, which of these options are going to, not only fill you up, but keep you fuller, longer? And, which option will take longer to eat?

Option B wins by a landslide.

And that, my friend, is why I'll never buy into the over-marketed, over-hyped, and frankly *dumb* "100-calorie" packs; 100 calories worth of pretzels is a joke.

Give me some substance, not hype. #GalaFortheGold

And. It's also why I'll never "get to know" Jenny Craig, either.

But, I do know eating smarter, outsmarting the marketing hype. And you do, too.

That's how you rise and hustle.

How to Pay it Forward

When I first started my online business, I was facing a demon.

Guilt.

Here's the back story: I was challenged by my mentor to give up things that took time away from my family or my business. That included cutting my grass. That meant, I was to hire someone else to do it. This felt odd. Here was a man roughly, 10 years older than me, outside in the Georgia heat, cutting my grass, while I worked on my business, in a comfortable air-conditioned home office.

In my head, I said: "This is so weird. I feel guilty."

Then it hit me...

I was investing this time back into my business, helping more people all over the world. In the meantime, someone that is better at cutting grass than I am [and much faster] was given a pay raise by adding my house to their business.

Not only was I investing my time into helping more people with my talents, someone else was able to provide more value with their talents.

My question to you is: *Why are you feeling guilty for your success?*

If you're experiencing growth and success by adding value to the world, there's nothing wrong with that. Hiring someone to do the things you're not good at or don't have time for is providing a job.

Nothing wrong with that, either.

Whether you're experiencing entrepreneurial success or got a promotion for your hard work, don't feel guilty about paying it forward.

That's why we rise and hustle.

I Got Into a Fight!

Just a few hours before the contract deadline to sell our old house, the potential buyer changed his mind on our agreed price and offered a whopping $13,000 less.

On top of that, as I was preparing for a Christian Writers Conference, I was putting out fires from my internet marketing business, and was smothered in distractions.

I couldn't help but ask, "Alright God, what are you up to? This is frustrating." Perhaps you can relate and you've asked the same question.

Well, the truth is, you and I should be flattered. The Enemy is jealous.

He sees that you're on the path to something much bigger than you could ever imagine. So what does he do? He points out the roadblocks in your life, to keep you from experiencing God's favor.

The closer you get to your breakthroughs, the more the Enemy will fight. Put on your boxing gloves. The Enemy fights with distractions, guilt, anxiety, and doubt.

Your weapon of choice? God's Word.

If the Enemy swings a right hook with doubt, duck and hit him back with Philippians 4:13 (NKJV): **I can do all things through Christ who strengthens me.**

If the Enemy attempts an upper cut with fear, swiftly lean back and then swing with Deuteronomy 31:6 (NASB): **Be strong and courageous, do not be afraid or tremble at them, for the LORD your God is the one who goes with you. He will not fail you or forsake you.**

When the Enemy throws a blow of distractions to keep you from achieving God's plans, look into his eyes and recite Isaiah 8:10 (NASB): **Devise a plan,** but it will be thwarted; State a proposal, but it will not stand, For God is with us.

Rise, hustle, and punch.

Three-Rant Rage

I'm still grumpy about the same things. This is based on a rant I wrote back in 2014 and these things still annoy me when it comes to our health. If you're sensitive, you may want to skip this. You've been warned.

Rant No. 1 "I Buy Them for the Kids"

Stop. Just stop it. The Oreos are as much yours as they are for your kids. The black crumble lips at 11:30 p.m. while watching Jimmy Fallon, are your lips or your kids' lips?

Oh snap.

Rant No. 2 You Buy Starbucks Coffee Almost Daily, But You Complain Healthy Food is Expensive?

I'll just leave that there. Defend yourself—please.

Exactly.

Rant No. 3 The Hideous, Annoying Scale Being the "Ultimate Tool" for Tracking Your Progress

I had one client that won a transformation contest, even with thousands of people voting. She went down two to three dress sizes, but only lost five pounds. At first, she was disappointed. But, when she finally realized it's possible to make a transformation without the scale changing, she was ecstatic. She understood what good health means and that it's more than what a scale says.

That's why I don't *understand*: "Mikey, my clothes are feeling looser and I have more energy than ever before. But, the scale hasn't changed. What am I doing wrong?"

Seriously. This is like winning $1.3 billion in the lottery and noticing that one of the bills has a crease in it [for crying out loud].

Stop measuring your progress with a scale.

Rant over. Today, rise, hustle, and keep going with no excuses.

Five Productivity Hacks for Busy People (Part One)

No. 1, I get my bad, corny jokes from my Mom. No. 2, I get my strong work ethic from my Dad.

No. 1 is an easy fix. I try to only say stuff like this to my wife, who can barely tolerate it:

"What do you call a sheep with no legs? A cloud."

Thanks Ma.

However, No. 2 can be tricky. Anyone can have a strong work ethic. Yet, you can work a full day with your sleeves rolled up and get your hands dirty—and *still* not get anything done.

It's called, *spinning your wheels*. Let's fix that.

No. 1 Your To-Do List Has 30 Things

It should only have three to five things on it. Your most important one or two "to-dos" should be worked on first, followed by one or two medium priority tasks, then one or two small tasks. This leads into my No. 2.

No. 2 Work On Your Most Important Tasks When You're "Into" It

My mentor and friend Craig Ballantyne calls this *magic time*; it's when you're the most creative. It's also when you can get three to four hours of work done in 90 minutes or less because you're focused. Feel less energized in the afternoon? That's when you work on the small tasks.

No. 3 Take Frequent Mental Breaks

It sounds counter-productive, but try this—every 90 minutes: Take three or five minutes to walk around or stretch. You'll come back a productive beast. It's like hitting a reset button. I personally play an epic game of "Hide-and-Go-Seek" with my black lab. This activity refuels me; satisfaction guaranteed.

No. 4 Check Your Inbox Twice a Day, Max

How many times do I have to say this? It's a game-changer, I'm telling you. If something is emailed to you at 10 am and you don't respond at 10:05 a.m., the world will carry on. Speaking of emails…

No. 5 Don't Check Your Email First Thing in the Morning

Work on your No. 1 priority *first* before checking your email. Email is nothing but a rabbit hole packed with distractions. Distractions keep you from doing the more important things.

To be continued…

Just like your desire to rise and hustle.

When the Bible Doesn't Work

You can read a book on making your lawn super green and thick, but it will still be brown and splotchy if you don't actually apply what you learn.

You can read, *How to Win Friends and Influence People*, but if you don't apply what you learn, you will still be avoided because of a sour attitude.

You can read powerful verses found in God's Word, but still have no change in your life because you don't apply what you learn.

For example, one of my favorite verses is Romans 12:2: **Do not conform to the pattern of this world, but be transformed by the renewing of your mind. Then you will be able to test and approve what God's will is—his good, pleasing and perfect will.**

If I read this, then go about my day with a negative attitude, conforming my standards to the world's standards—that doesn't really *do much good*. I'm betting I wouldn't see what God's will is for my life, either.

Perhaps that's why Matthew 25:21 says, **"Well done good and faithful servant."**

Notice it sure doesn't say, "Well known good and faithful servant."

Read *and apply* God's Word. That's how He desires you to rise and hustle.

Have You Gotten Your Y?

Back when I trained clients one-on-one, our first session was in the office. There wasn't any exercise at all. We sat and talked.

We mapped out three things:

1. Short-term goals
2. Long-term goals
3. The "Why"

Most people had no problem coming up with one and two, but when No. 3 came along, they stumbled.

You see, No. 3 is what really counts. This is what pulls you through the stubborn plateau you're bound to face. It's what pushes you to keep going when you mess up.

An answer to a specific "why" is what creates a magical motivation.

For example, let's say I asked a client why they wanted to lose 20 pounds over the next 12 weeks. And they reply with: *To feel better*—I would *yawn*.

I would dig deeper. *Why do you want to feel better?* After much thought (because they haven't thought about this before), they would give me specifics like*: So I can feel more confident in taking on important projects at work. Then, I would have the confidence to go after the management position I've always wanted.*

Ah, now we're getting somewhere. Magical motivation.

You see, my own "why" has everything to do with my two young sons, Champ [five] and Deakan [three]. I crave to chase them all over the house, hearing them laugh and scream at the same time. I don't want to be tired when I do this.

I want to take a spontaneous walk with them on a new trail so I can watch them throw rocks into a creek. I don't want to tell them, *maybe later. Daddy is tired right now.*

That's *my* why.

Take time to define *your* why and you'll find the motivation to rise and hustle, physically.

Three More for Busy People (Part Two)

I once knew a girl with two left feet. She wore flip-flips. That joke was so bad, it was a waste of your time, just like those silly meetings about the upcoming meeting in the corporate world. They ended up being complaining sessions about the lack of progress. If you suffer through this, I challenge you to ask if you can get a bulleted agenda before the meeting. If there isn't one—make one. You'll save yourself 45 minutes of pain. Meetings should include a decision. If not, they are a waste of time. That's *Bonus Hack No. 1* for really busy people, and you're welcome.

Hack No. 2 Build Blocks. Put down the Lego set. I'm talking about *time blocks*. I learned this from my mentor Craig Ballantyne. I did this for months to keep myself on track and productive. When it's time to work, you work. When it's time to play, you play. Here's a sample:

4 am: *Wake up + Quiet Time with God (My first meeting is with my CEO)*
4:30 am – 6 am: *Write*
6 am – 7 am: *Deal with emails + check in on my coaching groups on Facebook*
7 am – 11:30 am: *Work on a new product that I'm launching*
11:30 am – noon: *Eat*
Noon – 3 pm: *Continue working on the new product*
3 pm – 4 pm: *Emails, Facebook groups, and plan for next day*
4 am – 8 pm: *Family time followed by hitting the pillow at 8 pm*

Hack No. 3 Do Not Disturb. You can't get into a groove if your phone is constantly going off. Put it on Do Not Disturb mode when it's time to focus on an important project. If you're still tempted, put your phone in another room. It will be okay, I promise. You can't expect to make huge strides if your phone is going off every 10 minutes. We're not done yet, and you're not done rising and hustling.

Literally Walk Away from Your Rut

I remember going to my first Christian Writers Conference, stretching my entrepreneurial spirit and quite frankly, stretching my belly. In fact, one night at dinner, they served sweet potato casserole. It was so good; it made me cry.

A nice man was explaining his book to me, but the greatness of the casserole was so overwhelming, it was hard to concentrate. I kept singing in my head, "Then Sings My Belly... How Great Thou Art."

Let me ask you something: *Have you ever experienced a hard time concentrating when God is talking to you?*

Perhaps you've gone through something like this: You're having quiet time. There's not a single peep in the house. Yet, there is so much noise.

"What do I need to get done today?"
"Oh wow, I should work on that later."
"I wonder what we'll do this weekend."
"Ugh. That project is so frustrating!"

You name it. That's the Enemy trying to keep you from experiencing God's grace. *So what can you do?*

Walk.

Yep. Close your Bible. Walk out that door with no phone. Just walk and be open.

It's funny; people are willing to ask their friends, "Hey can we go for a walk and chat?" Yet, we're not willing to do the same with our Creator.

He'd love to go on a walk with you. A walk is where new ideas are born. Breakthroughs are made. "A-ha" moments are discovered.

If you find yourself in quiet time rut... walk it off for a new shake-up in your routine.

> **You shall walk in all the way that the Lord your God has**
> **commanded you, that you may live, and that it may**
> **go well with you, and that you may live long**
> **in the land that you shall possess.**
> —Deuteronomy 5:33 (ESV)

Take a walk, so God can guide your hustle.

Mistakes Make Great Stepping Stones

The problem: Perhaps over the weekend you ate a lot more than you planned to. Or, perhaps you skipped a workout here, and a workout there, the last couple of weeks.

The *wrong* solution: Be overwhelmed with guilt and beat yourself up over it.

Here's what happens when you do this: You then eat more because when you're stressed; that's what you do. That's what a lot of people do. It's a vicious roller coaster. Instead of beating yourself up, use these mistakes as stepping stones.

> *Don't carry your mistakes around with you. Instead, place them under your feet and use them as stepping stones. —Author Unknown*

There's a huge difference between "I can't believe I ate that much last weekend" and "Alright, my plan for this past weekend didn't work. I'm going to try something else next weekend so I don't make this mistake again."

It's almost like magic.

Your perception changes.

Your goals start to magically happen.

You start making progress, one stepping stone at a time.

It's also part of the "secret sauce" to your daily rise and hustle.

A Strange Way to Get "Unstuck"

Have you ever had a bad day? You know—one where you wish you could hit the reset button and start over? It seems like no matter how hard you work on a project, it just doesn't seem to get anywhere. You feel *stuck*.

Then, the frustration sets in and the rest of the day goes down the drain. The next thing you know, you're bullying your family and giving them a bad attitude, *just before dinner.*

There's an easy solution for this. Out of the blue, help someone else out. It sounds crazy—I know—but *it works*.

Hit a wall with your own project? Don't stress about it.

Reach out to someone and encourage them...

Ask them about their family...

Offer to swing by and drop off a chicken casserole...

Tell them a knock-knock joke...

Do something nice.

It's riveting.

For one thing, it distracts you from your own frustrations. Yet, the real "magic" happens when you return to your project. Suddenly, you find yourself with great clarity. Call it *goodwill voodoo*. It's crazy how well it works.

You'll be back in your groove before you know it. Then the next thing you know, you're rising and hustling.

Why is There Evil in the World?

It's the elephant in the room—the uncomfortable evil that perhaps smothers your social media feed: multiple shootings, kidnaps, abuse, trafficking. It's hard to inspire people while evil is at the forefront. But maybe—just maybe— I can find a way to encourage you while acknowledging this *elephant*.

Without a doubt, the Enemy wants us to point fingers and argue. Frankly, he's got us right where he wants us. He's enjoying us lash out at each other, instead of praying for one another.

> *This evil is breeding even more evil. I love it! —The Enemy*

Instead of praying for the families and friends of these precious victims, we take time to argue our points and to make sure we're heard. We want to prove our point all while the Enemy snickers in delight. Hey, I don't have the answers to overcome this evil in the world—that's why I'll be praying. I want God to help us find one.

I realize your argument might be, "Well Mikey, why does God let this happen in the first place?" Well my friend, you and I are free. We are not robots. God gave us free will to do what we want. Unfortunately, some people choose evil over love. There's no sugarcoating it.

It is absolutely clear that God has called you to a free life. Just make sure you don't use this freedom as an excuse to do whatever you want to do and destroy your freedom. Rather, use your freedom to serve one another in love; that's how freedom grows. For everything we know about God's Word is summed up in a single sentence: **Love others as you love yourself. That's an act of true freedom. If you bite and ravage each other, watch out—in no time at all you will be annihilating each other, and where will your precious freedom be then [Galatians 5:13-15 (MSG)]?**

And as for inspiration—it's found in Psalm 44:5 (GWT), **"With you we can walk over our enemies. With your name we can trample those who attack us."**

I will never stop praying. I will always have hope, no matter what the Enemy throws at us.

Rise and hustle among the chaos.

Why Sweat Doesn't Count

Back in the day, my personal training clients would question my approach. They would lose one or three pounds a week, yet they weren't convinced it was working.

The reason? They weren't sweating enough. They were concerned that the lack of sweat meant lack of results.

You see, that makes sense. After all, social media is flooded with women in sports bras, and men shirtless, pouring with sweat with the cliché sayings of "sweat if off" and other nonsense.

We're practically brainwashed into thinking our efforts are based on sweat.

I live in Georgia. On a random Tuesday afternoon, I could walk to my mailbox and come back into the house with my shirt drenched. That doesn't mean I had a great workout.

I guarantee you this—lifting up a few heavy things, and putting them back down will change your body faster, than running for an hour sweating your butt off.

And that, my friends, is why sweat doesn't count.

You know what *does* count? Your effort and diet.

You don't sweat eating healthy food, but it sure does change your body.

So sure, you can actually rise and hustle without sweating much... and completely transform your life.

Sweat or no sweat—that's how you rise and hustle.

Three Free Ways to Invest in Yourself

Wow, you won't believe this. I was at McDonald's the other day and I didn't realize how bad the economy has gotten. I overheard the employee ask a customer, "Can you afford fries with that?"

Hilarious. By the way, I'm kidding. I *never* go to McDonald's. I'm not lovin' it. And, as for the economy, I refuse to hear the negativity. Demonstrate and share value and you'll create your own economy.

Do you want to get better at that? Invest in yourself. "But Mikey, I'm broke." No problem. These are free—well, almost. You'll need to invest time. But, the good news is—time is free.

No. 1 Podcasts. Behold the power of podcasts. Whether you want to crush Facebook ads, speak better, write better, learn how to speak another language, or get inspired; there's a podcast for that. Sure, you can listen to immature "I got so drunk last night" stories on the radio instead, but that's your call.

No. 2 The Library. Yeah, they do exist and I go all the time. I'll even take my son Champ with me. Do you want to get better at something *really fast*? Read about it. You can't increase your value in this world by binging on Netflix. Read more. Learn more.

No. 3 Meet with Others. Did you know you're not the only one that wants to succeed at *stuff*? Want to lose weight? Find two or three other people (or more) who want to do the same. Help and encourage each other. Want to improve your business? Talk with other entrepreneurs. Share your victories and struggles. Want to get better at cooking? Start or join a cooking club. You get the idea.

Invest in yourself today to see the payoff tomorrow. That's how you rise and hustle.

The Race Before You

Are ready for the race ahead? Now let me warn you that you'll have mountains. You'll be climbing and wonder, "Is this ever going to end?" **Count it all joy, my brothers, when you meet trials of various kinds, for you know that the testing of your faith produces steadfastness. And let steadfastness have its full effect, that you may be perfect and complete, lacking in nothing [James 1:2-4].** Then suddenly, you'll be going downhill and everything will seem to be going easy. Enjoy it! **Also that everyone should eat and drink and take pleasure in all his toil—this is God's gift to man [Ecclesiastes 3:13 (ESV)].**

Look out for falling rocks out of nowhere. Distractions packed with guilt, doubt, fear, stress and busyness will fall from all directions. **We are hard pressed on every side, but not crushed; perplexed, but not in despair; persecuted, but not abandoned; struck down, but not destroyed [2 Corinthians 4:8-9].** Don't forget to rest as needed. Rest is part of the plan. **Come to me, all you who are weary and burdened, and I will give you rest [Matthew 11:28].**

Your race will be different than anyone else on Earth. God has called you for a specific purpose. No one else can do what you do. So stay focused on the race before you. **Therefore, since we are surrounded by such a huge crowd of witnesses to the life of faith, let us strip off every weight that slows us down, especially the sin that so easily trips us up. And let us run with endurance the race God has set before us. We do this by keeping our eyes on Jesus, the champion who initiates and perfects our faith. Because of the joy awaiting him, he endured the cross, disregarding its shame. Now he is seated in the place of honor beside God's throne. Think of all the hostility he endured from sinful people; then you won't become weary and give up. After all, you have not yet given your lives in your struggle against sin. [Hebrews 12:1-4 (NLT)].**

Keep rising. Keep hustling. Amen.

Don't Forget Your Free Resources

Reading *Rise and Hustle* is your first *big step* in transforming your life physically, personally, and spiritually.

Now for Step No.2...

The link below takes you to our FREE resources, which go along with the book. This includes:

- An easy-to-follow daily gratitude journal template to start your day off right.
- A simple five-minute accountability cheat sheet to get you in the best shape of your life.
- A cheat sheet of verses to read every day to keep an amazingly positive attitude.
- The seven-day jumpstart to change your life physically, personally, and spiritually.

Get all of these free tools when you visit:

http://riseandhustle.com/resources

About the Author

In 2003, Mike Whitfield started his own fitness journey by losing 115 pounds *and* keeping it off for 13 years. This propelled him into the fitness industry, allowing him to become a contributor to *Men's Health Big Book of Getting Abs* and being named Trainer of the Year twice, as well as Fitness Entrepreneur of the Year in 2013.

Whitfield's programs have helped tens of thousands of men and women transform their lives with his real, doable strategies. He has also spoken at several conferences on health, productivity, and building an online business.

Starting his own online business in 2011, his rapid success allowed him to step away from his personal training career after just four months. Six weeks later, his wife was able to quit her job as a teacher to become a Stay-at-home Mom.

However, it wasn't always this great.

Whitfield faced a dead-end job in the corporate world, questioning his purpose and even his existence. Years of obesity and low-esteem led to mild depression. He was also divorced from his high school sweetheart.

Now, living with passion and purpose, being happily married for 10+ years with two amazing boys, he has put together a book full of life's "mini-lessons" on how to become who God designed you to be. In this debut book, you'll truly learn how to #RiseandHustle in God's plan.

His followers know him as "Mikey Pancakes Whitfield" due to his love for pancakes. For authentic, doable advice, sprinkled with sarcasm and humor; guaranteed to transform your life physically, personally, and spiritually—for *free*, visit **www.RiseandHustle.com.**

 Morgan James makes all of our titles available through the Library for All Charity Organization.

www.LibraryForAll.org